The Focus on Democracy

The Grand Tour

The Focus on Democracy

Flavio Conti

Translated by Patrick Creagh

HBJ Press
a subsidiary of Harcourt Brace Jovanovich, Inc.
Boston

HBJ Press

President, Robert J. George

Publisher, Giles Kemp

Vice President, Richard S. Perkins, Jr.

Managing Director, Valerie S. Hopkins

Executive Editor, Marcia Heath

Series Editor, Carolyn Hall

Staff Editor, Chris Heath

Text Editors: John Bennet, Carole Cook,
Elizabeth S. Duvall, Judith E.
Hanhisalo, Amanda Heller, Joyce
Milton

Editorial Production: Karen E. English, Ann
McGrath, Eric Brus, Betsie Brownell,
Patricia Leal, Pamela George

Project Coordinator, Linda S. Behrens

Business Manager, Edward Koman

Marketing Director, John R. Whitman

Public Relations, Janet Schotta

Business Staff: Pamela Herlich, Joan Kenney

Architectural Consultant, Dennis J. DeWitt

Text Consultants: Janet Adams, Elizabeth R.
DeWitt, James Weirick

Design Implementation, Designworks

Rizzoli Editore

Authors of the Italian Edition: Dr. Flavio
Conti, G. M. Tabarelli, Daniele Riva

Idea and Realization, Harry C. Lindinger

General Supervisor, Luigi U. Re

Graphic Designer, Gerry Valsecchi

Coordinator, Vilma Maggioni

Editorial Supervisor, Gianfranco Malafarina

Research Organizer, Germano Facetti

U.S. Edition Coordinator, Natalie Danesi
Murray

Photography Credits:
Hornak: p. 73, p. 78, p. 79 top left, p. 79 bottom, p. 82,
p. 83 top, pp. 86–94, p. 96 / *Magnum:* p. 32 /
Magnum-Burri: pp. 153–157, pp. 159–164 / *Mairani:* p. 76
top, p. 76 bottom left, p. 81 bottom right / *Marka:* p. 13
bottom / *Marka-Huber:* p. 12 top, p. 19 / *Radici:* p. 18
top / *Radnicky:* pp. 57–68, pp. 105–116, p. 137, p. 140 top,
p. 140 bottom right, p. 141 right, pp. 142–148 /
Ricciarini-Cirani: p. 158 / *Ricciarini-Simion:* pp. 138–139 /
Ricciarini-Tomsich: p. 9 / *Rizzoli:* pp. 122–123 / *SEF:*
pp. 10–11, p. 12 bottom, p. 44 top, p. 76 bottom right, p.
79 top right, p. 121 / *Sheridan:* p. 13 top, p. 18 bottom,
p. 20 top, p. 21 bottom, pp. 22–23, p. 27 bottom right,
pp. 74–75, p. 77, p. 80, p. 81 top, p. 81 bottom left, p. 83
bottom left, p. 83 bottom right, pp. 84–85, p. 95 /
Tomsich: pp. 14–17, p. 20 center, p. 20 bottom, p. 21 top,
pp. 24–26, p. 27 top, p. 27 bottom left, pp. 28–31 /
Verkehrsverein: pp. 42–43 / *Visalli:* pp. 124–127, p. 132 /
Wagner: p. 140 bottom left, p. 141 left / *White House
Historical Association:* pp. 128–131 / *Widmer:* p. 41,
p. 44 bottom, pp. 45–52.

Library of Congress Catalog Card Number: 78-59729
ISBN: 0-15-003731-7

Printed in Hong Kong by Mandarin Publishers Limited

Contents

Preface

The Focus on Democracy

Our constitution is named a democracy, because it is in the hands not of a few but of the many. But our laws secure equal justice for all in their private disputes and our public opinion likes and honors talent in every branch of achievement, not for any sectional reason but on grounds of excellence alone. As we give free play to all in our public life, so we carry the same spirit into our daily relations with one another.

Thucydides
History of the Peloponnesian War
Book 2, Section 37

Thus, Pericles, the greatest statesman of ancient Athens, summed up the government of that small Greek city-state more than 2,500 years ago. Yet his words could equally apply to many other countries and many other historical periods—to the venerable Parliament of Great Britain, for instance, or to the founding of the Constitution of the United States of America.

Over the centuries, the concept of democracy has been expanded, so that today there are democracies of all sorts and interpretations. Even within the United States, democracy embraces both the New England town meeting, at which every citizen can have a say, and the Senate, where individual senators represent the states which elected them. All democracies, however, share a common insistence on the right and capacity of their people to govern themselves and to control their institutions for their own purposes.

In the Athens of Pericles, the whole citizen body formed the legislature. This system was possible because the population of the city rarely exceeded 10,000, and the majority were slaves, women, or noncitizens, who had no political rights. The leaders—sometimes elected, sometimes assigned by lot—were responsible directly to the people, who would crowd into the outdoor assembly place to carry out the business of government. In modern democracies, citizens are usually represented by elected officials, and the business of government takes place in town halls, parliaments, and other civic buildings, which often come to symbolize the whole democratic system. Indeed, they do not simply express a certain style or an architectural concept. Regardless of their age or aesthetic qualities, they communicate and embody a philosophy, an enduring aspiration, and a faith.

Our word "democracy" is a literal borrowing from the Greek "rule by the people." Yet Greek democracy has had little direct influence on modern democratic theory and practice. Contemporary democratic ideas evolved both from the philosophies and institutions of the Middle Ages, which stressed the reciprocal responsibility of ruler and ruled through divine and natural law and custom, and later from the enlightened intellectual and social ideas of the seventeenth and eighteenth centuries which brought about the American and French revolutions.

Pericles brought Athenian democracy to its zenith. Although its flowering constituted only a brief episode in the context of succeeding centuries of civilization, Pericles insured that it will never be forgotten. He enshrined the political and cultural pre-eminence of his city in some of the world's most magnificent buildings. The Acropolis, the rocky hill overlooking Athens that had already been for centuries the fortress and religious sanctuary of the city, had been devastated during the Persian Wars. Despite the vow the Athenians had made to leave the temples on the hill in their ruined state as an eternal memorial to that tragedy, Pericles commissioned the sculptor Phidias to rebuild them. Under Phidias' direction the greatest architects of the Greek world—Ictinus, Callicrates, and Mnesicles—set to work. Their buildings and temples conferred fame and honor on the city and all it stood for. The fragments and ruins that still stand, outlined against mountains and an azure sky, continue to reflect that same glory.

Equally well-known, and equally symbolic, are the Houses of Parliament in London. This site on the north bank of the Thames has been the center of the government of England for a thousand years. Here where the Lords and Commons now meet, Edward the Confessor built a royal palace, and in this spot the kings of England lived for five hundred years. But despite the existence of the monarchy, the government of Britain has evolved as a democracy ever since the days of King John, when his barons forced him to sign the Magna Carta in 1215. Only Westminster Hall remains of the original Gothic

Palace of Westminster, but the other buildings, although only a hundred years old, are also constructed in the traditional Gothic style.

The White House, residence and office of the president of the United States, is almost as old as the country which declared its independence from Britain in 1776 and went on to become the most powerful democracy in the world. At the same time as the swampy area bordering the Potomac River was being laid out as the Federal City, the simple and stately "President's palace," built in Virginia freestone, was constructed. Its design—that of a typical Georgian country mansion, with Palladian detail—owes much to Europe, but the eagle in stone relief above the entrance proclaims it as distinctly American. Since its construction, the White House and its inhabitants have played a central role in American life and history—particularly since the advent of radio and television. Uniting a country which spans a continent, the White House is the unassuming symbol of the fundamental principle, written by Thomas Jefferson, of the inalienable right of all Americans to "life, liberty, and the pursuit of happiness."

In Europe, democracy has taken many forms and followed unpredictable paths, from the democracy of the mountain cantons of Switzerland to that of the social and idealistic government of Sweden. Yet all the countries of the Continent solemnly acknowledge their debt to the past. Even in these days of centralized national government, town halls across Europe continue to evoke times of greater glory and importance.

Among these, the town halls of Antwerp in Belgium and Basel in Switzerland are particularly eloquent. Although Antwerp and Basel are not capital cities, their town halls recall the days when they were the centers of civic power in wealthy expanding cities, proud of their commerce and their independence. They remain symbols of that forceful and creative mercantile democracy which flourished throughout the Middle Ages and the Renaissance in the heart of Europe.

Although the Rathaus, or Town Hall, of Basel has seen extensive additions and renovations since its original cornerstone was laid in 1504, its architecture remains a distinctive combination of German late-Gothic and Italian Renaissance. Its modesty of scale, combined with its red frescoed walls, slender spire, and the elaborate clock on the façade, gives the building a toylike charm and intimacy which seems particularly Swiss. In comparison, the Flemish Renaissance architecture of the Stadhuis of Antwerp is grander and more opulently ornate. Built during Antwerp's heyday of prosperity and independence, it reflects the desires of the wealthy sixteenth-century burghers to embellish their city in a manner befitting such an important center of commerce.

The Stadshus of Stockholm differs somewhat from the town halls of Antwerp and Basel. For one thing, it is the town hall of a capital city. As such it represents not only the town of Stockholm but also the nation. For another thing, it is more modern. Designed by the Swedish architect Ragnar Östberg, it was only completed in 1923. The massive building of natural red brick standing at the edge of Lake Mälar is a monument to the Swedish national character and history. Its tall square bell tower, which dominates both the building and the Stockholm skyline, harks back to the Middle Ages, recalling the days when a tower was a prominent symbol of civic independence and prerogative. Swedish materials were used in the construction of the building and gardens, and Sweden's mythical and historical heritage is commemorated in statues, monuments, paintings, and mosaics.

Throughout Europe's history, there has been a strong link between freedom and sea trade. Democracy has often evolved within societies of traders. Certainly this seems true of Denmark. Early in the seventeenth century, the vigorous Danish King Christian IV transformed the quiet medieval town of Copenhagen into a large and well-protected port. In addition to building strong fortifications, he founded the Børsen, or exchange. The Børsen is a long narrow building, conveniently adjacent to a canal, in which merchants once carried on a lively trade in commodities and luxury goods. Today it is still in use, but now only stocks and shares are exchanged within its walls. Crowned by a fantastic spire composed of the entwined tails of four dragons, the Børsen symbolizes not only the mercantile spirit but also the mythical seafaring heritage of the kingdom of Denmark.

Europe's long history is evoked in almost all its public buildings. But when in the 1950s the then-democratic government of Brazil decided to build a new capital city, they were looking not to past glories but to an optimistic future of unrealized possibilities. In contrast to the colorful coastal city of Rio, Brasília, six hundred miles into the hinterland, is a monument to modernity. Vast skyscrapers, domes, and housing complexes flanking a wide mall four and a half miles long characterize this much-maligned metropolis. Many people have criticized Brasília's cold and inhuman atmosphere. Yet these monoliths succeed—where perhaps more conventional buildings might have failed—in asserting an undeniably contemporary vision in the middle of the immense tropical savanna.

Varied as the buildings in this volume are, they are united by a common cause. Each is in its own way the concrete expression of an abstract ideal, honoring or illuminating the democratic principle. The words of Pericles, echoing down the centuries, are as inspiring and relevant today as they were to the Athenians of the fifth century B.C.

The Acropolis

Athens, Greece

The Acropolis of Athens is a craggy, walled hill. It was for centuries the citadel of Athens, in addition to being the home of Athena, patron goddess of the city. Originally, the Acropolis also contained the chief municipal buildings of the city, but later it became an exclusively religious sanctuary.

Preceding page, the Acropolis, dominated by the Parthenon (to the right), the Erechtheum (center), and the Propylaea, or gateway (left). The little Temple of Athena Nike is next to the stairway leading to the Propylaea. In the foreground is the Theater of Herodes Atticus, built in the reign of the Roman Emperor Marcus Aurelius. Above left, the west side of the Acropolis. Left and right, the Propylaea, the monumental entrance to the Acropolis, viewed from the hillside approach below. Above right, a distant view of the Propylaea, the Erechtheum, and the Theater of Herodes Atticus.

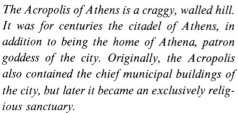

Right, the Ionic Temple of Athena Nike, or
Athena of Victory, built on the southwest flank
of the Acropolis beside the Propylaea. Planned
by Callicrates, the temple was erected in commemoration of the peace of 421 B.C. Dismantled
by the Turks in 1686 to make room for a gun
emplacement, the temple was reconstructed in-
accurately by archaeologists in the last century
and then later rebuilt more correctly. It is considered a superb example of the Ionic style.
Above, one of the Ionic capitals and the architrave and frieze of the Temple of Athena Nike.
Left, the base of a monument erected in the second century B.C. to celebrate a royal victory in a
chariot race. Under Roman rule it supported
statues of Antony and Cleopatra and later one of
Marcus Agrippa, friend and son-in-law of the
Emperor Augustus.

Left, the Propylaea—the only opening in the wall surrounding the Acropolis—and the remains of the Panathenaic Way which zigzagged up the hillside. During the Persian invasion of 480 B.C., work on an earlier monumental entrance to the Acropolis was destroyed. During the years 437 to 432 B.C., the architect Mnesicles rebuilt the entrance in its present form, with a Doric exterior and Ionic interior. To the right of the Propylaea is the Temple of Athena Nike.

Inside the left wing of the Propylaea (above) was the Pinakotheke, the earliest known instance of a room designed expressly as a picture gallery. Above right, the Propylaea viewed from atop the Acropolis.

Right, the Erechtheum, seen through the central passageway of the Propylaea. Every few years, the Panathenaea, a huge festival in honor of Athena, was held, and a great procession climbed the sacred way to the Acropolis and passed through the Propylaea. To accommodate the large numbers of people and vehicles, the columns of the central passage were more widely spaced than the others.

Left, the finely dressed marble exterior columns of the Propylaea. Doric in style, they appear massive and a little primitive in comparison with the slender, refined Ionic columns of the Temple of Athena Nike (above) and of the interior of the Propylaea (right). Beside the columns stand two huge column drums with the characteristic dowel holes in their centers.

The Parthenon, the temple dedicated to the cult of Athena Parthenos, or Athena the Virgin, was built by Ictinus and Callicrates, under the supervision of the sculptor Phidias, between 447 and 432 B.C. The present sense of its openness, especially at the eastern end (top and center left), is a result of a gunpowder explosion which occurred during the Venetian bombardment of the Turkish-held Acropolis in 1687. Most of the interior cella walls were blown out, and only the western part still remains (bottom left). The Parthenon was originally painted and decorated with bronze accessories. In the early nineteenth century, Lord Elgin, the British ambassador to the Ottoman Empire, removed a large part of the extant pediment sculpture of the Parthenon. Known ever since as the Elgin Marbles, they are now in the British Museum.

Right, above and below, the western façade of the Parthenon. The temple was built in the most archaic and conservative of Greek styles—the Doric—and is unrivaled in the purity and refinement of its lines. All the major horizontal lines of the temple are slightly curved, possibly in an attempt to give life to its geometric perfection, or perhaps to counteract the distortions of perspective that occur in viewing a large building. Yet the Parthenon also embodies some notable deviations from the norm. For instance, it is eight columns wide and seventeen columns long instead of the traditional six by thirteen, and the columns are somewhat closer together than in most Doric temples.

The arches in the foreground (below right), part of the Theater of Herodes Atticus, are Roman. The Greeks understood the principle of the arch well enough to have employed it occasionally in their sewers, but they never accepted it as being worthy of inclusion within their traditional system of architecture.

Following page, the Parthenon as it appears from near the Propylaea. Like all Greek temples, the Parthenon was intended to be experienced as a harmonious sculpture in space, viewed primarily from the outside and from every angle.

Although the Parthenon represents the ultimate refinement of the Doric temple, the sculptural friezes depicting the Panathenaic procession, which stand over the inner end colonnades and cella walls (above left), are more typical of the later, more elaborate Ionic order. The characteristic alteration of triglyphs—projecting blocks ornamented with three vertical channels—and sculpted metopes (below, above, and above right) and the severe fluted Doric columns (right and bottom row left) are a direct translation into stone of archaic wood and terra-cotta temple elements. The fluting of the columns also emphasizes their verticality by creating vertical highlights and shadows. Above, a corner of the eastern façade, with copies of some of the original pediment sculptures. The originals are the so-called Elgin Marbles in the British Museum. Above right and below, lion-headed rainspouts on two other corners of the Parthenon.

Above, the Erechtheum, with its slender scroll-topped Ionic columns, and modern Athens in the background. Although this asymmetrical cluster of porticoes and porches appears disorganized, almost un-Greek, it may originally have been intended to be symmetrical. According to one theory, the famous caryatid porch facing the Parthenon on the south side and the Ionic porch which stands in line with it facing Athens on the north side (left, above right, below near right) were to have been the centerpieces of a symmetrical double temple. Below far right, the strangely filled-in western colonnade of the temple.

Although the Greek orders were highly standardized, the details of the porch of the Erechtheum (top) are noticeably more delicate than those of the eastern portico (immediately above). The small holes in the frieze originally held metal pegs which fastened lighter colored marble figures to the darker gray marble background.

Right, with details far right, the Porch of the Maidens, whose graceful caryatids—statue-columns derived from archaic votive figures—face toward the Parthenon.

Just below the Acropolis lies the Theater of Dionysus, as later modified by the Romans (above left). The theater could hold more than 10,000 people. The marble chairs of the front row were reserved for the priests of Dionysus. Below far left, Silenus, the tutor of Dionysus, crouching at the base of the stage. Below near left, one of the most elaborate of the marble seats, its legs shaped like lion's paws.

Above, the agora, or civic center, of Athens overlooked by the Temple of Hephaestus, the oldest surviving marble Greek temple. Below left, some of the columns of the Temple of Olympian Zeus. Begun by Peisistratus in the sixth century B.C., the temple was not completed until the second century A.D. by the Roman Emperor Hadrian. Below right, the remains of the colonnade which surrounded the Roman agora.

Following page, the Acropolis, seen from the Hill of the Muses to the southwest.

The Acropolis Athens, Greece

"There is but one entry to the Acropolis. It affords no other, being precipitous throughout and having a strong wall. The gateway has a roof of white marble, and down to the present day it is unrivaled for the beauty and size of its stones." Such were the admiring comments of the Greek traveler Pausanius in the second century A.D., writing of the sacred rock that dominates Athens. For more than two millenniums, visitors have been awed by the Athenian Acropolis, which represents the essence of Classical Greek architecture. Rarely have the works of man and nature been so powerfully combined: the severe perfection of the Parthenon, the unexpected complexities of the Propylaea, the graceful yet austere Erechtheum, and the delicate Temple of Athena Nike. These

are the legacy of the Golden Age of Athens, tributes to one of the most glorious eras in architectural history.

The name "acropolis" means "high city," indicating the defensible hilltop sanctuary around which Greek cities often developed. Many of these cities began as nothing more than an area of high ground surrounded by a crude barrier that enclosed the huts of the people and a somewhat grander hut for their leader. Over the centuries, however, the Athenian Acropolis came to be considered sacred. It was surrounded by sophisticated fortifications and reserved for temples and statues celebrating the local deities. Except in time of war, the common people lived outside its walls.

The Acropolis that towers over Athens is a small plateau 900 feet long and 300 feet wide, rising almost 800 feet above sea level. Its eastern and southeastern sides are sheer precipices, forming natural walls that were extended artificially. Since the northern face is also steep and hazardous, the only possible approach is from the west.

At least seven thousand years ago, this hilltop was inhabited by a race of farmers

who had domestic animals and who used tools of stone and bone. They were called Pelasgians by the later Greeks. Originally from Thessaly, a region in what is today northern central Greece, these Neolithic farmers had gradually migrated to the mountainous, sometimes fertile, land farther south. Some chose to remain in Attica, the region of ancient Greece where Athens was situated.

The Pelasgians chose one of the smallest of Attica's rocky outcrops for their settlement—according to legend, an abode of snakes and owls. They drove away the snakes but let the owls remain. As late as the Classical period, the owl was still venerated and was often represented on Athenian coins.

Apart from such tales, little is known of early Greece until the second millennium B.C. when the Myceneans arrived. They were wealthy traders, whose tombs contain Minoan vases from Crete, wine from Phoenicia, and scarabs from Egypt. They may even have imported their rulers, for it is said that the first kings of Attica were Egyptians—Cecrops and his successor, Erechtheus. More likely, these kings were not native Egyptians but Indo-European Hyksos, a people who had for a time con-

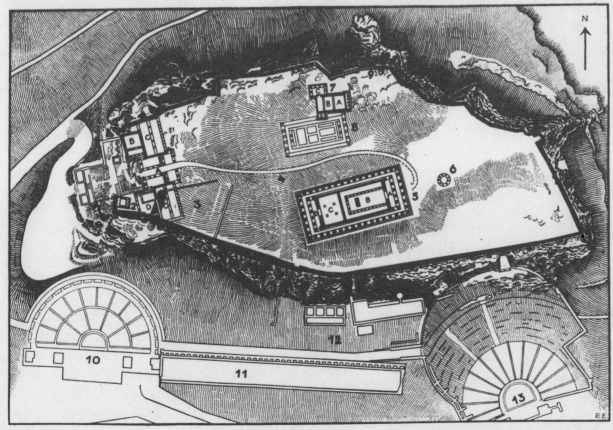

Left, plan of the Acropolis:
1. Propylaea
1B. Pinakotheke
2. Temple of Athena Nike
3. Precinct of Artemis Brauronia
4. Panathenaic Way
5. Parthenon
6. Temple of Rome and Augustus
7. Erechtheum
8. Foundations of the Old Temple of Athena
9. Location of drums of columns of the previous temple
10. Roman Theater of Herodes Atticus
11. Stoa of Eumenes
12. Asclepeum
13. Theater of Dionysus

Above, Solon, Athenian legislator of the sixth century B.C.

Right, Athena receiving homage from craftsmen.

Below, two didrachmons, Athenian coins with Athena's head on the obverse and the Athenian owl on the verso.

quered the Nile Valley. Later driven from Egypt, some of the Hyksos emigrated to Greece where, with the wealth and experience they brought from more civilized lands, they swiftly gained power. Cecrops is credited with civilizing the Athenians to the extent of instituting marriage and abolishing all forms of blood sacrifice.

Legends from this period abound. During the reign of Cecrops (ca. 1581 B.C.), Athena is supposed to have fought Poseidon for possession of Attica. After the people nominated her the victor, gracious Athena presented them with the olive tree, which was thereafter considered sacred. The arrogant loser Poseidon struck the rock of the Acropolis with his trident, but he only succeeded in bringing forth a useless spring of salt water.

The cult of Athena became the principal religion of the city. The lesser deities of neighboring villages were absorbed into the cult, and common worship created a single community called Athenai, derived from the Pelasgian, meaning "the united communities of Athena." From this time, late in the second millennium B.C., Athe-

nian civilization began to spread, although the Acropolis remained its citadel as well as the sanctuary of the gods.

Around 1300–1225 B.C., the top of the Acropolis was leveled and surrounded by walls that the later Greeks called Cyclopean—suggesting that only the giant one-eyed Cyclops could have moved such huge blocks of stone. Thanks to these fortifications, Athens was the only city of Greece to withstand the Dorian invasion of the eleventh century B.C. Legend, however, attributes the victory of Athens to a less prosaic cause. One oracle proclaimed that the Dorians would defeat Athens—but only if they spared the life of Codrus, its king. When the king learned of this prophecy, he stole into the enemy camp disguised as a beggar and provoked a fight, in which he was killed. After they realized what they had done, the invaders withdrew.

It is also said that the self-sacrifice of this exemplary king marked the beginning of democracy in Athens. The people, feeling that no king could equal Codrus, were said to have replaced the monarchy with a government overseen by nine elected officials, called archons. Although this early form of democracy was not instituted as a regular system until 682 B.C., nearly four hundred years after the death of King Codrus, the legend dignifies the beginning of what was to become one of the most magnificent epochs in human history.

Thucydides, the great Athenian historian, attributed the power of Athens to the poverty of its soil. The land's infertility, he said, discouraged the invaders who periodically overran the rest of Greece; as a result, Athens became a refuge for the most powerful citizens of other states. Certainly, the soil's barrenness encouraged Athens's drive toward colonial expansion. As early as the beginning of the Iron Age (ca. 1100 B.C.), waves of refugees were causing serious overpopulation in Attica, and the Athenians were already devoting their energies to colonization.

The Greek states and the Persian Empire were engaged in a series of conflicts in the first half of the fifth century B.C. In 480

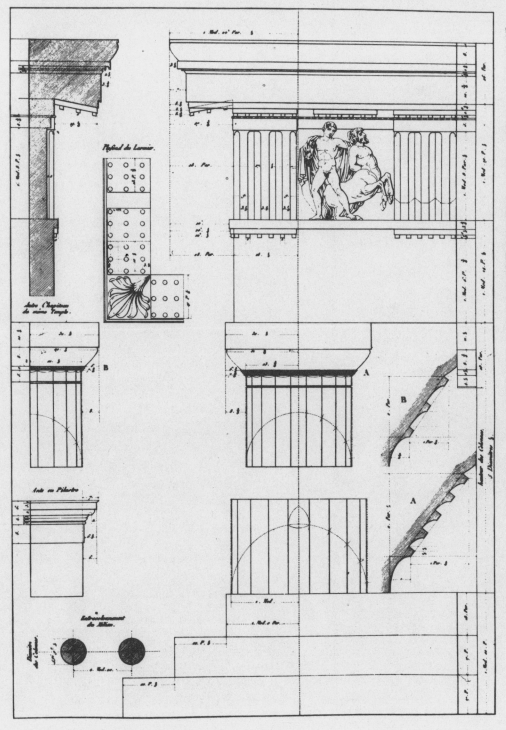

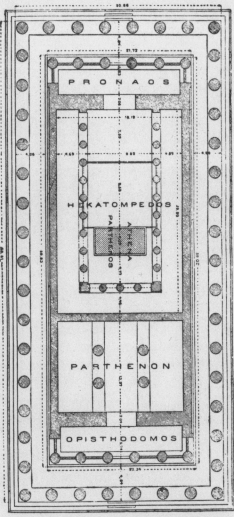

Left, details of the Parthenon, from the bottom up: stylobate, column, capital, architrave, frieze, and cornice. The Parthenon represents the high point of the Doric order. Above, ground plan of the Parthenon. Its original name—Hecatompedon (100 feet) refers to the length of the interior chamber.

B.C., during one of these Persian Wars, Athens was taken by the enemy. A Greek traitor had guided the Persian army through the mountains to the narrow pass of Thermopylae, which was defended by Leonidas, king of Sparta, and three hundred followers. Leonidas heroically held back the Persians, but his troops were eventually surrounded and trapped by a Persian detachment. They chose to die fighting rather than to flee.

The Persians then descended on Athens and seized the Acropolis, putting an end to the thousand-year-old legend that it was impregnable. Xerxes ordered the city to be burnt to the ground. Among the buildings destroyed on the Acropolis was the great temple to Athena Parthenos (Athena the Virgin Warrior), which the Athenians had built on the site of an older and smaller sanctuary to consecrate their victory over Xerxes' father, Darius, at Marathon ten years earlier. The temple is one of the most magnificent examples of early Classical architecture.

When the Persians had finished, all that remained was the marble base of the temple, blackened by flames. The Athenians were so demoralized by this loss that they swore they would never rebuild the temples of the Acropolis. They resolved to let them remain exactly as the Persian troops had left them—shattered and charred.

Athens was at last led to victory over the Persians by Pericles, a popular statesman and orator. An ardent patriot, Pericles was more interested in a bright future than a glorious past, and he brought the city out of the war as the mistress of an empire and leader of half the Greek states. His empire was held together by a fleet of two hundred warships built to defeat the Persians.

Below, an ostrakon, *or potsherd, bearing the name of Aristides, one of the ten generals who commanded the Athenians at Marathon. He was ostracized—condemned to exile by popular vote—for opposing the naval policy of the powerful Athenian statesman Themistocles. Right, details of the Erechtheum, showing the subtle differences between the various Ionic porches and porticoes of this temple.*

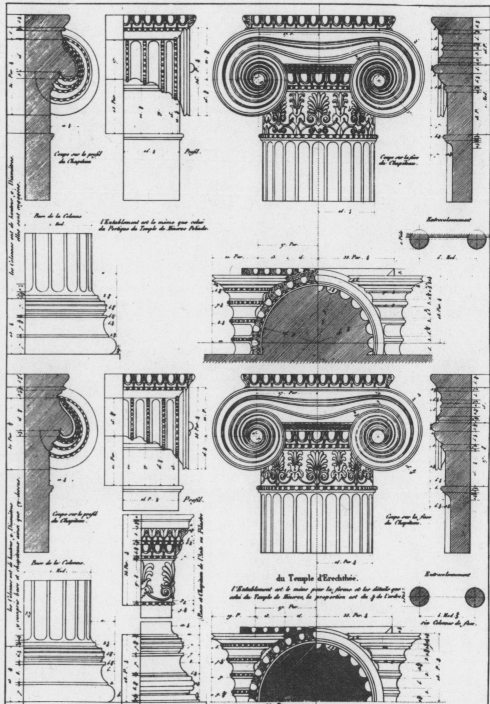

In the wake of victory came tribute money from the subservient Greek states and a healthy economy based on new markets and growing prestige. However, the Greek alliance occasioned by a common enemy would have to be maintained in times of peace by other means.

Pericles turned to art and civic grandeur as a means of reinforcing the power of Athens. Even then, Athens was a flourishing center of architecture, sculpture, and ceramics. Temples such as that of Athena Polias, a celebrated example of early Doric architecture, had been erected. In the fifth and sixth centuries, there had also been considerable technical and aesthetic development in the field of sculpture. During that period, Athenian sculptors were beginning to work in bronze and to cast life-sized statues which were the first realistic depictions of human anatomy.

To gain the admiration and respect of the Greek peoples, Pericles determined to rebuild the Acropolis. He wished to endow it with the highest achievements of human genius, the most beautiful temples, and the richest and most harmonious buildings and statues. The Acropolis was to be the symbol of Athenian democracy and the hub of the empire. Pericles' vision included rebuilding dend enlarging both the great Temple of Athena Parthenos and the Propylaea, the gateway to the plateau. He also planned for other buildings, sanctuaries, and statues as well as a theater for music, the Odeum.

In return for the protection from the Persians provided by the Athenian fleet, Athens's Greek allies were to bear the immense cost of the project. The treasury established on Delos for the military expenses of the confederation was appropriated by the Athenians, who thus increased their wealth by 30 million drachmas (equivalent in value to eleven tons of gold). The confederation was required to allocate an additional 18 million drachmas when the construction was well-advanced.

The allies of Athens did not take kindly

to this use of their money. In the words of Thucydides, they were outraged that "their contributions, extorted from them by force for the war against Persia, should be used by the Athenians to gild and embellish their own city, making her appear in the eye of all like a harlot with precious stones, statues and temples costing a thousand talents." These resentments grew, feeding the rivalry that was to break out in the Peloponnesian War. But for the moment Pericles prevailed.

His reconstruction of the Acropolis was the biggest single building program in the

Above, Themistocles, the brilliant general and politician who saved Athens from the Persians at the Battle of Salamis. Above right, Pericles, who governed Athens during its Golden Age. Right, Alcibiades, whose political maneuverings are sometimes blamed for the fall of Athens. Below, a reconstruction of the western pediment of the original Hecatompedon of Pisistratus. Two lions growl fiercely over a captured wild bull.

history of Athens. To direct the work, Pericles chose Phidias, Ictinus, Callicrates, and Mnesicles. Phidias, who was to supervise the project and coordinate the various programs, had learned to paint from his father, the artist Charmides. He soon turned, however, to sculpture, an area in which his supremacy was to remain unchallenged for nearly two thousand years—until the time of Michelangelo. Working on a grand scale, Phidias managed not only to preserve the correct proportions of his figures but also to imbue them with an inimitable air of serenity.

The architects Ictinus and Callicrates were charged with rebuilding the Temple of Athena Parthenos. Then known as the Hecatompedon ("of one hundred feet") because of its width, it is today called the Parthenon ("the maiden's chamber"). Mnesicles is known to be the architect of the great gateway, the Propylaea, and of a group of smaller sanctuaries called the Erechtheum.

Architecture, to the Greeks, meant more than simply designing buildings. Rather, it was the unity between the man-made and the natural, for the landscape

itself was considered a vital element of architecture. Buildings were arranged to incorporate or accentuate—often from afar—natural features of the mountainous environment, creating a composition that was unified and balanced in space.

The Acropolis, like other holy places in ancient Greece, had been held sacred long before it became the site of temples and religious monuments and statues. Certain conformations of plains, hills, and mountains, illuminated by the magical effects of Greek sunlight, seem to have had a special appeal for the Greeks—possibly because they evoked images of human forms. These places, it was believed, were a congruence of sacred and natural forces. They became, first, places of sanctuary, and eventually the site of buildings dedicated to the gods.

Our concept of architectural space—that which is constructed and enclosed—was not shared by the Greeks. For them, space was defined by the balance between the landscape, the buildings (especially sacred ones), and the people who inhabited them. A twentieth-century Greek architect, Constantinos Doxiadis, suggested that the ancient Greeks' sense of space in design was based on their theories of optics. He identifies the focal point of the Acropolis—the single point about which it was designed and from which it must be understood—as a spot just inside the Propylaea. Here one would first experience, in a single balanced view, all the major monuments on the plateau. And just as the eye was made to understand the relationship between them, so too the landscape of the buildings itself was arranged to lead one among the structures in a way that seemed both natural and ritually appropriate.

Dominating this scene was the Parthenon. Built between 448 and 432 B.C., this temple was the only one of Pericles' monuments to be completed before the Peloponnesian War put an end to all construction. Like all Greek temples, it was meant primarily to be seen from the outside. Viewed from the city below, it dominates the landscape, standing out against the sky like a ship on the sea. Through an illusion of setting and perspective, the Parthenon does not recede into the distance. Instead, it projects its colonnaded sides, seeming to turn them toward the viewer. Always changing, as if in continuous motion against its background, it epitomizes the Greek sense of architecture.

The Parthenon represents the ultimate refinement of the Doric temple. Built of golden Pentelic marble, it is 228 feet long by 101 feet wide and 65 feet in height. The columns, which number eight instead of the more traditional six on the ends, and seventeen rather than thirteen on the sides, enclose a large, rectangular block, called the cella, which is divided into two spaces: the traditional sanctuary where the statue of Athena stood, and behind it a smaller depository for ceremonial objects called the Parthenon—which has now lent its name to the building as a whole.

In the Parthenon, graceful architectural refinements are worked on the austere Doric order to give the temple uniquely light and elegant proportions, which are especially remarkable in view of the size of the building. The long, horizontal lines of the temple, the stylobate supporting the columns, and the architrave frieze and cornice above them are also slightly curved, so that they are somewhat higher at the center than at the ends. Possibly the architects hoped, in this way, to counteract the tendency of the eye to see long, straight lines as if they sag slightly. Or they may have wished to lend a certain life and vitality to what they might have feared to be the temple's otherwise deathly perfection. For presumably similar reasons, the columns lean slightly inward, and the intervals between the final columns are slightly narrower than the others—this last, probably, to compensate for their being

Near left, a miniature dating from the second century B.C. of the colossal gold and ivory image of Athena made by Phidias for the Parthenon. The statue cost almost as much as the Parthenon itself.

Above far left, the orator Demosthenes. This is a Roman copy of a statue made by Polyleuktos in the third century B.C. Below far left, the orator Aeschines, political opponent of Demosthenes. He was forced into exile in 330 B.C.

seen against the bright sky instead of the dark cella wall. All of these deviations from the apparent simplicity of the temple's Doric order required a remarkable attention to detail. For example, every capital of the colonnade is different from the next, in order to fit the curvature of the architrave.

Construction of the Parthenon entailed tremendous technical problems. Twenty-two thousand tons of marble had to be moved by sled from the quarries across ten miles of plain, through the city, and up the steep slopes of the Acropolis. Roads were rebuilt to bear the weight; even so, the blocks were only moved in summer for fear of getting them stuck in the mud. Moving one block of marble from the quarry to the Acropolis took at least two days and cost up to 300 drachmas, at a time when one drachma was the average workman's daily wage. Each of the Parthenon's 35-foot columns was assembled in sections and then fluted in place, a procedure learned from the Egyptians. Indeed, the Greeks had probably learned the art of building temples—and the mathematics that made it possible—from Egypt.

Although we now admire the building for the purity of its honey-colored marble, red, black, ocher, and blue paint was originally used to pick out the sculpted reliefs and certain architectural details. In the cella stood an immense statue of the goddess Athena, the masterpiece of Phidias. The almost 40-foot-high statue was made of gold plates supported by a wooden armature. It was both a religious and economic symbol of Athens, containing as it did the gold reserves of the state. The plates were easily removed, both so that they could be hidden in times of strife and so that the magistrates could check their weight.

Around the outside of the cella ran a continuous frieze in low relief. It was carved on marble slabs over 3 feet high and up to 14 feet long, with figures cut in 1¼-inch relief at the bottom, then graduated to 2¼-inch at the top to compensate for the steep angle of vision from which it is seen. The frieze depicts the most important religious ceremony in an-

Right, a drawing of the Catastrophe of the Year 1687, *showing the fallen columns of the Parthenon. Shells from Venetian cannon, seen in a contemporary engraving (below), detonated a supply of gunpowder which the Turks, who held the city, had stored in the temple.*

VEDUTA DEL CAST: D'ACROPOLIS DALLA PARTE DI TRAMONTANA.

cient Athens, the Panathenaea. The birthday of the goddess Athena, the Panathenaea was celebrated in July. Every fourth year this festival was especially splendid, centering around a great procession of participants bearing a woven robe for the goddess. The participants in the ceremony—the horsemen, the maidens, the elders, and the youths—are carved on the frieze. These figures have a solemn beauty and grace that have never been equaled.

The Propylaea, the entrance to the Acropolis, was begun in 437 B.C. by Mnesicles, but work was halted by the outbreak of the Peloponnesian War in 431

B.C. Extending over the entire western face of the Acropolis, the Propylaea had an imposing central gateway with a wing on either side. Visitors approaching the Acropolis passed through the western portico of the central gateway and, after climbing six steps, reached the eastern portico. The two central columns in each portico were spaced widely enough to permit the passage of vehicles in processions. Of the intended rooms within the wings, only one—in the northern wing—was completed. This was the *pinakotheke*, or picture gallery, the first room known to have been constructed solely for the display of paintings.

The little Temple of Athena Nike (Athena of Victory), just outside the Propylaea, was built from Callicrates' design in 427–424 B.C. The Athenians dedicated the temple to their hope for a naval victory over Sparta. Built entirely of Pentelic marble, the temple's only decoration was an Ionic frieze, of which only fragments remain. Around 408 B.C., the Athenians surrounded the temple with a protective parapet of marble blocks decorated with reliefs of Athena Nike.

The Erechtheum, on the northern edge of the Acropolis, was probably another of Pericles' projects, although it was not begun until 421 B.C., eight years after his death. Purportedly named for the legendary King Erechtheus, it stands on the spot where the mythical battle between Athena and Poseidon is said to have taken place.

The architect Mnesicles was charged with replacing the ancient sanctuary of Athena Polias, which had been destroyed by the Persians, without disturbing the sacred site. The new temple, with its tall, slender Ionic columns, was built to accommodate several different cults. It also had to serve its various religious purposes without distracting from the adjacent Parthenon. It succeeds through contrast. The Erechtheum is certainly one of the most original buildings of the Classical age. With the white marble figures of its frieze thrown into sharp relief against a darker background of gray Eleusinian marble, its asymmetrical plan—possibly not originally intended—and its air of delicacy and brilliance, the Erechtheum is the perfect complement to the massive grandeur and dignity of the Doric Parthenon.

By the time that construction of the Erechtheum was under way, the brief Golden Age of Athens was coming to an end. The Peloponnesian War, begun in 431 B.C., was to destroy the Athenian empire and overwhelm the democratic government of the city. But the Acropolis, the high rock dedicated to the gods and to the achievements of a brilliant era, remained throughout the centuries to kindle the spirit of man. As Thucydides wrote with pride: "If the city of Sparta were to be destroyed, and there remained only the temples and the foundations of the buildings, men of later ages would be very incredulous of its power and fame.... Whereas if the same thing were to happen to Athens, from the look of the city posterity might suppose that it was twice as powerful as it really was."

Twenty-five centuries have passed over the walls of the Acropolis. Macedonians, Romans, Byzantines, Franks, Catalans, Florentines, and Turks have ruled them. Much of its sculpture was carried off to England, and most of the rest is kept in Greek museums to save it from air pollution. The Erechtheum has been a Catholic church and a harem. The Temple of Athena Nike was demolished for a gun emplacement and had to be reconstructed twice by archaeologists. The Parthenon has been a church, an Orthodox cathedral, a mosque, and finally an arsenal. This last use proved to be its ruin, for Venetian ships attacking Athens in 1687 fired on it, blowing up its store of gunpowder. The explosions shattered twenty-eight of the columns—many of which have since been re-erected—blew out the walls of the cella, brought down the architrave and much of the frieze, and scattered the roof over the countryside.

One of the most impressive monuments to man's greatness thus became a monument to his stupidity. But as long as human dignity, creative ability, national pride, and the love of beauty have any meaning, they will be embodied in the Parthenon.

Below, a drawing of the Acropolis dated 1670. The battlemented tower on top of the Propylaea had been erected by the Franks, while the minaret next to the Parthenon—which was a mosque at the time—was built by the Turks.

The Rathaus

Basel, Switzerland

The brightly painted Rathaus, or Town Hall, in Basel, Switzerland, presides over the city's centuries-old Marktplatz, a thriving open-air market (preceding page). The town grew up where the Birsig River flowed into the Rhine—a natural place for a trading center. When not occupied by outdoor vendors, the marketplace doubles as a parking lot (above).

The red frescoed façade of the Rathaus (left) provides modern visitors with an idea of what much of Basel looked like in the sixteenth century. The original building extended only the width of the three great arches. (An open ground-level arcade was a traditional, almost emblematic, component of such civic structures.) The Front Chancellery on the left was finished in 1608, and the two flanking neo-Gothic extensions were added in the late nineteenth century. Restored in 1901, the original façade (right) is a surprisingly compatible marriage of late-Gothic architectural components—the tall windows, pointed arches, and elaborately ornamented clock—and the painted Renaissance decorative elements.

RENOVATVM ET AMPLI
FICATVM ANNO DOMINI
MDCCCCI

RENOVATUM ET AMPLI
FICATUM ANNO DOMINI
MDCCCCI

Flags and coats of arms are favorite decorative motifs in Switzerland. Three soldiers guard the splendid clock (below left) made by Master Wilhelm in 1512. The standard-bearer holding aloft the banner of Basel is a copy of the original which is now in the city's historical museum. The figures flanking the canopy just above the clock, sculpted by Hans Thurner in 1511, represent the city's patron saints, Henry II, Holy Roman Emperor, and his wife Kunigunde. The figure between them was originally the Madonna, but after the Reformation in 1608, her scepter and child were replaced by a sword and scales, and she is now known as Justice.

The frescoed façade on the original sections of the Rathaus (detail, above far left) employs in two dimensions the architectural vocabulary of the Renaissance—including window pediments and a balcony—all rendered in correct perspective. Above near left, an ornate bay window which adorns one of the nineteenth-century wings of the Town Hall. Its sinuous grapevine ornamentation reflects the influence of the German Art Nouveau.

The Romantic neo-Gothic additions to the Rathaus include the colorful tiled roofs and the high tower with its bells and crowning pinnacles (right). These nineteenth-century additions appear even more Gothic than the earlier building that inspired them, in the sense that they more closely meet the standards of the Gothic followed during the high Middle Ages. A reptile perched atop a drainpipe (below) and the ranks of small grotesques which enliven the vertical moldings between the windows of the courtyard (below right) are typical of the nineteenth-century additions.

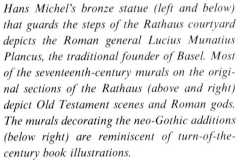

Hans Michel's bronze statue (left and below) that guards the steps of the Rathaus courtyard depicts the Roman general Lucius Munatius Plancus, the traditional founder of Basel. Most of the seventeenth-century murals on the original sections of the Rathaus (above and right) depict Old Testament scenes and Roman gods. The murals decorating the neo-Gothic additions (below right) are reminiscent of turn-of-the-century book illustrations.

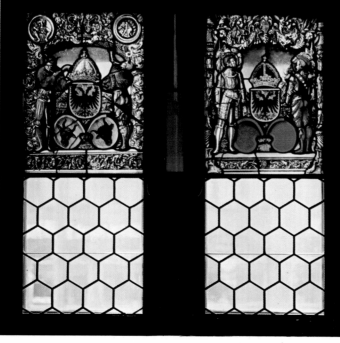

The Council Chamber (above left) is, apart from the great U-shaped table of the councilors, a remarkably coherent example of a German late-Gothic room. The room is completely paneled and is decorated with masterful woodcarving throughout.

Below far left, two of the leaded windows in the Council Chamber, decorated with brilliantly colored stained-glass panels. To the left is the coat of arms of the Swiss canton of Uri and on the right, that of the canton of Schwyz. The work is attributed to Anthoni Glaser (1521).

Below near left, a small segment of the Upside Down World, an intricately carved wooden frieze by Hans der Bildschnyder based on a sketch by Israhel von Meckenem. The work spans the Council Chamber ceiling.

The original council table, now kept in another room, was carved by Johann Christian Frisch in 1675. In return for his work, Frisch was granted citizenship in Basel. Each leg of the table (above near right) depicts a pair of monsters, basilisks, putti, or lions clasping the shield of Basel and supporting the table top on their heads.

Franz Pergo, who became a burgher of Basel in 1593, executed the Council Chamber's Mannerist grand portal (below right) in 1595. The room's only Classical intrusion, it is crowned by two basilisks supporting the city shield and flanked by the symbols of Justice and Fortitude.

Above far right, one of the two carved busts, depicting unidentified prophets, which flank the portal. Their creator, Martin Hoffman, was attracted to Basel by its reputation as a center of Renaissance humanism but was reduced to making his living as an ordinary carpenter by the iconoclastic attitude of the Reformation. He subsequently returned to his home in northern Germany.

The Rathaus of Basel (following page) lies at the heart of a city which is itself a vital commercial and industrial center of Europe.

The Rathaus
Basel, Switzerland

Unlike many other town halls, which today exist only as museums, the Rathaus of Basel is in its fifth century of use. The business of the city is still carried on within its frescoed walls, a tradition that commemorates the continuing prosperity of this proud and ancient Swiss city.

Since its cornerstone was laid in 1504, the Rathaus has grown, as one scholar described it, like a tree, with roots, a trunk, branches, and leaves. The building was actually modified in two distinct stages: One annex, the so-called Front Chancellery, was added a century after the original building was completed, and at the beginning of the twentieth century, the whole was thoroughly restored and enlarged with two more flanking wings, one of which was a tower. The evolution of the

Rathaus thus mirrors the steady cultural and commercial growth of Basel, a town that began as a modest trade settlement on the banks of the Rhine.

The first-time visitor to Basel is often astonished to learn that the city is a citadel of wealth. It is commonly said that more than half of Switzerland's many millionaires are Baselers. Conservatism, which often accompanies wealth, has always been a strong Swiss trait. Display of any kind is regarded as a sign of poor taste; pretension is a heinous offense. Such a natural character could explain the distinct lack of grandeur typical of Swiss architecture, including Basel's Rathaus. What others might regard as humble, the Swiss are inclined to commend.

Basel's wealth and eminence grew steadily over the centuries, primarily because of its fortunate geographic position. The city is situated at the juncture of the borders of Switzerland, France, and the Black Forest of Germany—about a mile down river from where the Rhine first becomes navigable. For centuries, travelers seeking passage from the north through the mountains to the Mediterranean took advantage of the Rhine's opening in the Jura Mountains. Medieval Basel thus

stood at the crossroads of Europe. For this reason, it was a natural choice for the Council of Basel, which drew learned theologians, priests, bishops, and abbots from all over Europe to debate troublesome questions concerning the organization of the Church. After the council was finally adjourned in 1449, the town fathers moved to maintain the intellectual tradition established by the council and, at the same time, responded to the economic deficiencies caused by the departure of the council members by establishing the University of Basel. This institution, the first of its kind in Switzerland, was destined to become one of the most prestigious in Europe, and Basel became one of the centers of Renaissance humanism in Europe.

From the beginning of the fifth century, Basel was ruled by a succession of bishopprinces. But at about the same time that

Basel was one of the richest, most strategically located cities in sixteenth-century Switzerland. Below, a print by Hans Asper depicting the city in 1548. The Rhine still divides the city into the port of Kleinbasel in the north (far side) and the older Grossbasel to the south. Below left, a sixteenth-century drawing of a standard-bearer attributed to Hans Holbein the Younger.

Monumental frescoes by the great Renaissance portraitist Hans Holbein the Younger once decorated the walls of the Great Council Chamber of the Rathaus. But by the end of the sixteenth century they had deteriorated completely. Today all that remains are a few fragments and some original preliminary drawings. Above, The Anger of King Rehoboam. *Left,* King Shapur Humiliating the Emperor Valerian, *which is made to take place in front of Basel's Rathaus as it looked before the façades were frescoed and the addition of the Front Chancellery blocked the arch on the left.*

Above, four surviving fragments of Holbein's murals depicting elders and councilors. Below right, Holbein's portrait of Erasmus. Below left, the artist's self-portrait in a guildmaster's robes.

the original four cantons of the Swiss Confederation signed their initial alliance against their imperial Hapsburg overlords (1291), the thriving merchants and guildmasters of Basel began, little by little, to take over—and at times to buy—the temporal rights and privileges of the bishops. By the fifteenth century, the burghers were in firm control of their government, and the Swiss Confederation eagerly invited the Baselers to join them.

With Basel's acceptance by the Swiss Confederation in 1501, the Town Hall then in use no longer adequately represented the prestige, wealth, and spirit of the city. Nor was this the first time that Basel had had to replace its Rathaus. The earliest one stood at the quay on the Rhine, the second on the present site of the town's Marktplatz, followed by a third destroyed by an earthquake in 1356. Basel's new Rathaus, the heart of

today's structure, was begun in 1504. The structure was built during Basel's golden age, a time when the city was an important European center of commerce as well as of art, academic learning, fine printing, and publishing. It was in Basel that Hans Holbein the Younger first learned his trade and made his reputation. It was also in Basel that Erasmus of Rotterdam took refuge from the excesses of the Reformation. In Basel, Erasmus began his fruitful partnership with the publishing house of Johann Froben in 1514. Their editorial collaboration secured not only Froben's fame as a publisher of scholarly texts but also the Church's acceptance of Erasmus' intellectual independence. In 1521, after Luther's condemnation at the Diet of Worms, Erasmus took up permanent residence with Froben, who introduced the scholar to his protégé, Hans Holbein. Out of this relationship came the series of por-

traits on which the modern conception of Erasmus—his frailty, his noble spirituality, his dedication to scholarship—is based.

When Holbein first arrived in Basel, the main elements of the Rathaus had been completed. The new structure was an example of the secular, late-Gothic style that developed in Germany in response to the rise of an urban middle class, overlaid with Italian Renaissance details. The Gothic is apparent in the grotesque heads supporting the arched "cornice," the shield-bedecked battlement immediately above it, the turreted canopy over the clock, and the slender and delicate spire astride the roof. The Renaissance features, on the other hand—although perhaps more immediately striking—are all merely painted on the flat surfaces of the façade. They include such architectural elements as the pediments that crown the large second-story windows as well as the human

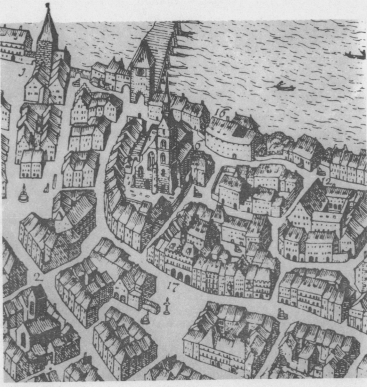

Left, the still-unpainted façade of the old Rathaus as it looked shortly after its completion in 1514. Above, a seventeenth-century illustration of Basel showing the Rathaus and Marktplatz (number 17).

figures above them.

The Rathaus was the collective work of many of Basel's finest guildmasters. The original plans were apparently developed by a man named Ruman Fasch. The elaborate clock on the façade is attributed to Master Wilhelm and the turret to Diebold von Arx. The intricate latticework inside the arches of the three front portals is a later work of Hans Diebolder.

Guarding the façade of the Rathaus is the carved standard-bearer who carries the flag of the city of Basel in affirmation of Swiss pride in battle. Swiss history is rich in stories about individuals and small bands of soldiers—usually mercenaries—who held their ground against insurmountable odds. One of the more famous recounts the bravery of the Swiss Guard's defense of the Tuileries Palace in Paris on August 10, 1792, during the French Revolution. Some five hundred Swiss were massacred trying to save Louis XVI from the rage of his own people. Another episode maintains that a Frenchman once reproached a Swiss soldier for fighting for money. "And what do you fight for?" asked the Swiss. "For honor!" insisted the Frenchman. "Oh well," was the reply, "each fights for what he has not got."

Hans Thurner's statues within the canopy that crowns the Rathaus clock also reveal an aspect of the Swiss character. The two flanking figures represent Emperor Henry II and his wife Kunigunde, the patron saints of the city. The middle figure originally depicted a Virgin and Child, but in 1608, the passionate religious convictions of the Reformation prompted the substitution of a sword and scales for the child, thereby transforming the statue into a representation of Justice.

The elaborately painted façade of the Rathaus is not merely a superficial attempt to keep up with the times but is also characteristically Swiss and represents a long-standing tradition throughout Germanic Europe. Even Hans Holbein, before establishing himself as a portraitist, painted several houses in Lucerne and Basel. It was these notably successful commissions, along with the recommendation of his patron Jacob Meyer, then mayor of Basel, that secured Holbein an opportunity to paint the three wall murals in the newly completed Great Council Chamber.

Holbein gave the poorly lighted room the appearance of an open portico by dividing the walls with pilasters, columns, and statues in niches and treating the intervening spaces as apertures through which open-air scenes could be seen. The subjects for these grotesque and bloody representations of ancient political demeanor were meant to alert the purveyors of justice to the dangers of corruption. They were suggested by Beatus Rhenanus, a close friend of Erasmus, but their vivid pessimism about human nature belongs to Holbein alone.

The first two walls were completed by the autumn of 1522, but the dismissal of Mayor Meyer and uneasy political conditions halted the work. The third wall, painted between June and September of 1530 after Holbein's return from his first

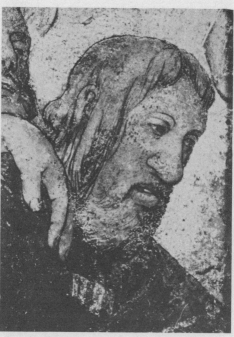

Above left, an engraving by Jacob Meyer in 1651 of the city's bustling market square and the Rathaus just to the right of center. Left, a drawing made in 1825 showing the structure and decoration of the lower part of the Rathaus façade. Above, detail of Holbein's fresco Rehoboam, which once decorated the Great Council Chamber.

trip to England, is said to have reflected both the new religious ideas and Holbein's mature style. Tragically, the murals deteriorated beyond repair over the next fifty years because the plaster walls had not been prepared properly. The original sketches and the few fragments of the murals that may still be seen today in Basel's art museum convey a frustrating sense of irreparable loss. One cannot help feeling that Holbein's work must have been the crowning achievement of the sixteenth-century Rathaus.

With a simple symmetry emphasized by the ornamental clock and turret above the middle of its triple, ground-floor arcade, this oldest part of the Rathaus measured only 59 feet wide. In 1608, the addition of the so-called Front Chancellery on the north side of the Town Hall permanently altered the simplicity and symmetry of the building. Nearly three centuries later, be-

tween 1898 and 1904, the aging Rathaus was thoroughly restored and enlarged by the two self-consciously Germanic structures on either side of the façade.

What was new disguised itself as old. And what was old was restored beyond its original glory into an idealization of itself. This sort of overenthusiastic restoration work is condemned in our own time. In the case of the Rathaus, many of the restorations were undone in the late 1940s. Yet the neo-Gothic additions to the Rathaus succeeded in continuing a tradition of organic development that harks back to the building's origin. This makes it easier to accept the fact that the architects enlarged the Rathaus—so that it might continue to serve its modern democratic city—without doing violence to the original building.

Despite these comparatively large additions, Basel's Rathaus remains intimate and inviting. This almost homelike build-

ing is far from the grand conceptions of the town halls of Antwerp and a hundred other Northern European cities—buildings which, to varying degrees, seem to reflect the prosperity more than the sensitivity of their builders.

The architectural values woven into Basel's Rathaus say much about the Swiss. For centuries, their small confederation of states has witnessed the rise and fall of empires. It has survived the wars of the Protestant Reformation, the tumult of the French Revolution, the Napoleonic Wars. It maintained its enviable state of neutrality when all Europe was ravaged by two world wars, and today its government and its currency are comforting testimonies to stability in an unstable world. So too has Basel's Rathaus tenaciously retained its place as the center of its government, adapting itself to centuries of religious, political, and economic change.

The Børsen

Copenhagen, Denmark

Preceding page, the southern façade of the Børsen, the exchange of Copenhagen. The Børsen was begun in 1619 by the colorful King Christian IV, who was seeking to promote and increase Danish trade. Somewhat ironically, the style of the exchange is strongly Dutch Renaissance—the native style of Holland, Denmark's primary sea-trading rival of the time. Bought in 1856 by the Society of Wholesale Merchants and now restored, the Børsen is the oldest such building still in use.

The 176-foot copper spire of the Børsen (right), composed of the entwined tails of four dragons, was designed in 1625 by L. Heidritter. Copenhagen is a city of copper spires (above), but the distinctive form of the dragon spire has no parallels in Northern Europe. It provides a strong vertical emphasis on an otherwise horizontal building. The weather vane which surmounts the spire was a help in former times in predicting the arrival of ships in the harbor.

Left, the northern façade of the Børsen. Ships were able to dock in the adjacent canal and unload directly into the building.

A sandstone parapet encloses a funnel-shaped court (below left) that leads to the western façade of the Børsen (left). The elements framing the door, including the "correct" Tuscan Doric columns, constitute a typical Renaissance frontispiece, but the rounded volutes incorporated into the medieval stepped gables (right) are evidence that the inspiration for the building as a whole came to Denmark by way of the Netherlands. The façade is guarded by a statue of Neptune (below) by I. C. Petzold. Beyond the north side of the Børsen, in the distance, rises the tower of the Christiansborg Palace (above), now occupied by Denmark's Parliament, Supreme Court, and Foreign Office.

The red brick façades of the Børsen are ornamented with a grid of horizontal and vertical elements, including hundreds of male and female half-figures on the pilasters (below and far left). The massive octagonal copper drum (near left) which supports the dragon spire contrasts with the curiously delicate gables. Although the gables are Classical in style, their spirit is almost Gothic. Such contrasts are typical of the work of Lorentz and Hans van Steenwinkel, the Flemish architects who designed the Børsen for Christian IV.

Right, a statue inspired by the ancient Roman deity Laverna, goddess of wealth, which surmounts the west gable. Below right, one of the carved heads that decorate the pediments of the ground-floor shop windows of the Børsen.

The interiors of the Børsen reflect the venerable traditions of Danish commerce. Top left, the modern library of the Børsen. Center far left, some of the gilded leather covering the walls of the Great Hall. A similar leather covering lines the President's Room (above right) which contains a portrait of Christian IV. The king is also commemorated in a statue by Bertel Thorvaldsen, which stands in the Great Hall (center near left).

Immediately below, an eighteenth-century ornate gold clock depicting the Børsen and the adjacent canal; bottom, a model of a merchant's ship. Both clock and ship are kept in the museum of the exchange.

Below far left, a twentieth-century mosaic showing the many spires of Copenhagen. Below right, the modern Conference Room lined with portraits of the past presidents of the Børsen.

The Børsen Copenhagen, Denmark

Few countries can claim as many imaginative legends and myths as Denmark and its capital Copenhagen. From the earliest Norse myths emerged Viking sagas recounting tales of fierce piratelike warriors who ravaged the coastline of Northern Europe in their longships, from the eighth to the tenth centuries. Many centuries later, the Danish author Hans Christian Andersen christened his country the "Land of the Storks." Good luck is still said to come to those houses where these once-numerous birds nest. Andersen's *Fairy Tales,* written in 1835, continues to be cherished the world over, and a bronze

statue of his melancholy little mermaid stands near the harbor in Copenhagen. The fanciful spires and towers atop Copenhagen's buildings also cast an enchanting, almost magical, mood, particularly the entwined dragon tails that crown the famous Børsen, or exchange, in the center of the city.

The idea for the Børsen was conceived by the resourceful Danish King Christian IV, who also served as designer, architect, and engineer for the building. Christian inherited the throne in 1588 when he was only eleven but did not begin to rule until he came of age in 1596. He was a vigorous, pleasure-loving man, fond of physical activity of all kinds. Christian's swashbuckling, energetic character made him one of the most popular of Danish kings—despite his military record. He not only led two unsuccessful campaigns against Sweden, in the hopes of uniting that country with his own, but also brought further disaster on Denmark in 1624, when he embroiled his country in the Thirty Years' War.

In times of peace, Christian occupied himself with the economic and cultural development of his kingdom. His avid interest in shipbuilding occasioned the en-

largement and improvement of the Danish fleet. Similarly, his admiration for architecture was manifested throughout the many new towns Christian founded for trade, and particularly in his capital Copenhagen, which he transformed from a provincial town into a handsome and dignified city embellished with imposing Renaissance buildings.

The city of Copenhagen, often referred to as the "Paris of the North," already had a long history when Christian IV ascended the throne. As early as A.D. 900, a Viking fishing village known as Havn (meaning harbor) existed on the site. The settlement grew into a trading center and came to be called Køpmannhavn, or Merchant's Harbor. The town received its first royal charter in 1422, and by 1443, it was the acknowledged capital of the kingdom of Denmark, which then included Norway and some of the Baltic states.

Below, an early engraving (ca. 1610) of Copenhagen. Known from the Middle Ages as the Merchant's Harbor, the city became Denmark's capital in the fifteenth century and a commercial center under Christian IV in the seventeenth century.

HAFNIA METROPOLIS ET PORTVS CELEBERRIMVS DANIÆ

COPPEN HAGEN

1. Das Königliche Schloß.　2. Vnſer Lieben Frawen　3. S Peter　4. Heilig Geiſt Kirch.　5. S. Nicolai Kirch.　6. Die Inſul Axelhues darauf das Kön Zeughauß.

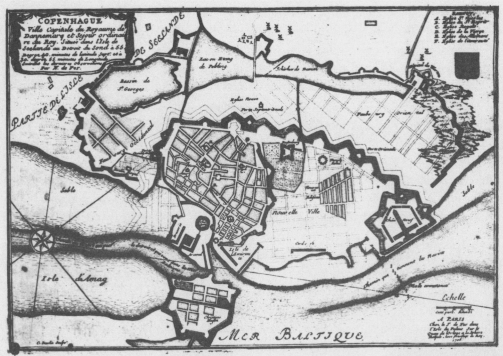

By the early seventeenth century, when Christian began to enlarge Copenhagen, it had become a flourishing community. The original town lay along the eastern shores of the island of Zealand, separated by a narrow strip of water (the Kalvebod) from the island of Amager, which had been settled by the Dutch for a century. Christian's plan was to build a new quarter on the other side of the channel. Almost a new city, it would be connected to the old town center by a bridge erected in 1618.

Christianshavn, as it was christened by the king, was constructed primarily to encourage Danish merchants to expand their commercial activities, in an attempt to rival the economic power of the Dutch. Considerable growth also occurred north of the original town, in the area then known as New Copenhagen, but now called Frederikstad. Christian also began to surround both Christianshavn and the expanding Copenhagen with massive fortifications that proved impregnable for almost two centuries. The Kalvebod provided a perfect harbor and Danish commerce accommodated a growing trade in agricultural produce and Icelandic goods.

As Christian was directing Copenhagen's expansion, he was also enthusiastically directing the construction of numerous buildings in and around Copen-

Above, a French map (1706) showing the fortifications of Copenhagen, Christianshavn, and New Copenhagen. Expansion into the latter two areas was initiated by Christian IV (above right). Right, the chapel of Christian IV in Roskilde Cathedral, built by Lorentz van Steenwinkel. The statue of Christian to the right is by Bertel Thorvaldsen.

hagen, one of which was the king's "gay summer house." Though primarily designed by the architect Bertel Lange, Christian himself took a hand in planning and laying out the grounds, still called the King's Gardens. This red-brick Scandinavian Renaissance palace was the site of much festivity and celebration—led by the hard-drinking Christian—and remains a monument to that lively period of Denmark's history.

In the Børsen, Copenhagen's exchange, Christian cleverly combined his enthusiasm for building with his desire to boost Copenhagen's already prosperous commerce. Begun in 1619, the long, narrow structure was adjacent to the harbor and flanked by two canals. As its inscription says, the bourse was "founded by His Majesty not for the secret rites of Laverna and Mercury, but for the glory of God and profitable use by buyers and sellers." It served as a place where local merchants and foreign traders could carry on their business and is now the world's oldest continuously operating trade center.

Christian may have conceived the idea for such a building during a visit in 1606 with his sister Anne, wife of England's King James I. It is probable that he was inspired by the London Royal Exchange, which provided him with an impressive model for an exchange in Copenhagen. Like much of the architecture sponsored by Christian IV, the Børsen reflects the concepts of the Italian Renaissance, as it

The canals of Copenhagen, seen in these nineteenth-century views of the city (top and center right), provided easy transport of goods to the Børsen. Although many goods were sold in the bourse, there were also—and still are—numerous open-air markets (bottom).

came to Denmark via the Netherlands after the mid-sixteenth century. The designers of the Børsen were two of King Christian's most trusted architects, the Flemish brothers Lorentz and Hans van Steenwinkel.

The elaborate end portals of the Børsen are adorned with columns and pilasters carrying correct Classical capitals, while the elongated, narrow sides exhibit a businesslike regularity in the even spacing of doors and windows and also in the rows of pediments that order the red brick walls. The nine gables also provide a firm rhythm along the roof. Conventional "crowstep" construction was abandoned on these gables in favor of their more voluptuous outline and bands.

The most immediately striking feature of the Børsen is the imaginative ornamental spire that crowns the copper tower of the building. The spire was designed in 1625 by Ludwig Heidritter, and it is said that Christian IV worked on the construction with his own hands. A remarkable piece of craftsmanship, it consists of the intertwined tails of four dragons. Although it is evidently influenced by current Mannerist developments in Italy, it is distinctly northern in spirit.

The interior of the Børsen is as elaborate as its exterior. Ships were able to tie up at the adjacent wharf and unload directly into the ground-floor shops, where everyday goods were offered for sale. Additional merchandise could be hoisted into the attic. The principal floor—above the level of the shops—was reserved for luxury merchandise. Not just goods but also news and gossip were exchanged here, between fishwives and sailors as much as merchants and businessmen.

The Børsen was a lively, noisy place, a combination of shopping center, newsroom, and dock. Amidst the din of vendors crying their wares and arguing

A century ago, ship owners and bankers thronged the main hall of the Børsen (left). Today, most transactions are conducted electronically.

Left, a nineteenth-century photograph of the main entrance to the principal floor of the Børsen. The exterior of the exchange has remained basically unchanged since 1625.

over prices, drunken sailors—home for the first time in months—would quarrel over the women who ran their own, less legitimate businesses. The King's Guard, proud of their Vandyke beards and flowing moustaches, would march ostentatiously through the bourse, their drums and trumpets attracting the attention of local beauties. The Børsen was unquestionably a roaring success.

For a time, Christian was able to enjoy the profits of his venture, which had cost him a great deal of money as well as effort. Eventually, though, he was forced to give the building to a rich merchant named Peder Madsen in payment of a debt. Madsen owned the bourse only until the reign of Frederick III, Christian's son and successor, when it was reacquired by the throne in a calculated move toward absolute monarchy.

Danish trade thrived under the new political system, which brought stability to a country plagued by Baltic wars and class struggles. For a few years after the French Revolution, Copenhagen served as a major commercial center. But this pros-

perity ended during the Napoleonic Wars, when Denmark, under the guidance of Frederick VI, signed an armed-neutrality pact with Russia, Sweden, and Prussia to protect Baltic interests. In 1801, the British navy bombarded Copenhagen's harbor and, despite a valiant defense, the Danish fleet was destroyed—a crippling blow to the country's economy. By 1814, the state was bankrupt and a private bank had to be established to handle government funds.

Denmark's economy eventually began to recover, and in 1856, the Børsen—by then serving largely as a stock exchange—was bought by the powerful and ancient Society of Wholesale Merchants, who almost immediately elected to renovate its interior.

Yet a few testimonies to the old days remain. Trading is still vigorous, although only stocks and shares now change hands. The price of Danish butter continues to be set every Thursday. And a statue of Christian IV gazes proudly over the bustling stock exchange, a reminder that it was largely his vision which created a vital economy in a country with so few natural resources. Copenhagen is now the capital of a country with one of the highest incomes in Europe, and the Børsen is still in "profitable use by buyers and sellers."

Houses of Parliament

Preceding page and left, the Houses of Parliament and Westminster Bridge, seen from the south bank of the Thames. The Parliament building dates only from the nineteenth century. It was designed by Sir Charles Barry to replace the venerable Palace of Westminster, which was all but destroyed by fire in 1834. The palace was a rambling complex of buildings, accommodating many law courts as well as the House of Lords and the House of Commons. These buildings had grown up over the centuries around the medieval Westminster Hall, which survived the fire.

The committee in charge of the design competition for the new Parliament buildings stipulated that only entries in the Gothic or the Elizabethan styles would be considered. Barry's winning entry included a number of drawings by Augustus Pugin, a young artist in the vanguard of the neo-Gothic movement. Pugin's remarkable sketches reproduced in minute detail typical authentic Gothic decorations. The building, richly decorated with Pugin's spires, pinnacles, and tracery (below), is dominated by its clock tower known as Big Ben (right) and by the Victoria Tower, which serves as Parliament's archives (below left).

The clock tower of the Houses of Parliament is one of the most familiar sights in London (left). The tower, 320 feet high, houses Big Ben, a great bell weighing thirteen tons. First cast in 1856, the bell owes its nickname to Sir Benjamin Hall, chairman of the construction committee. Though strictly speaking the name belongs to the bell, it is often applied to the clock as well.

Above left, the gable of St. Stephen's Porch; above right, the Victoria Tower flying the Union Jack; and below, the New Palace Yard looking toward the north end of the medieval Westminster Hall.

The Houses of Parliament display a remarkable wealth of neo-Gothic decoration, including spires and towers (top left and above), statues in niches (center left), floral designs, and the heraldic device of the lion and the unicorn, symbolizing Britain (bottom left). Lions especially are a popular decorative theme (above far right and near right).

Far right, a cast of Rodin's Burghers of Calais, *which stands in the adjacent Victoria Tower Gardens. It commemorates the six elders of that city who surrendered to Edward III of England in 1347 in order to spare the lives of their fellow townsmen. The original statue stands before the town hall in Calais.*

THE BURGHERS OF CALAIS
BY AUGUSTE RODIN

The interior and exterior decorations of the Houses of Parliament constitute a history of the English nation and represent all the major protagonists of the long history of Great Britain. Left, a statue of Richard the Lion-Hearted by Marochetti (1860), which stands in the Old Palace Yard, one of the two forecourts.

The House of Lords and the House of Commons are surrounded by a series of rooms called lobbies in which Members of Parliament may meet with constituents or colleagues who hope to persuade (or "lobby") them on a particular issue. Statues of two great twentieth-century prime ministers, Winston Churchill and David Lloyd George, flank the fire-scarred entrance from the Commons Lobby to the Commons (right). Below left, the Commons Corridor looking from the octagonal Central Lobby toward the Commons Lobby and the Commons. Below right, the Noes Lobby, into which the Opposition retires at voting time.

St. Stephen's Hall (above left and above) connects the Central Lobby (below left and facing page) with St. Stephen's Porch. In ceremonial spaces such as these, Pugin gave Parliament a setting of Gothic splendor such as it had never known in the Middle Ages, with vaulted roofs, heraldic windows, mosaics, and other rich neo-Gothic embellishments.

Following page, the interior of the House of Commons. Burned out in a bombing raid during World War II, the House was redesigned in a toned-down neo-Gothic style by Sir Gilbert Scott in the late 1940s. The red stripes on the floor serve to separate the Government from the Opposition.

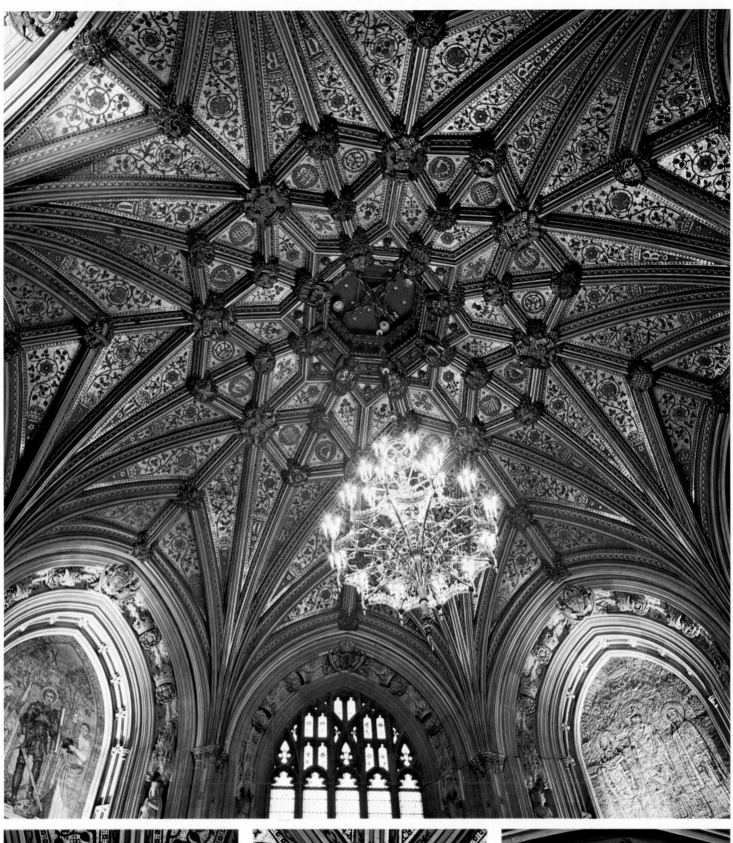

Compared to the austere Commons, the richly decorated House of Lords seems a suitable setting for the peers of the realm who gather there. The decoration is chiefly the work of Augustus Pugin, who also supervised much of its execution. Above, the House seen from the gallery behind the throne. Left, the gallery reserved for visitors and journalists. Right, the rear wall of the Lords. In front of the throne, which was inspired by the Coronation Chair, is the woolsack, the traditional seat of the Lord Chancellor.

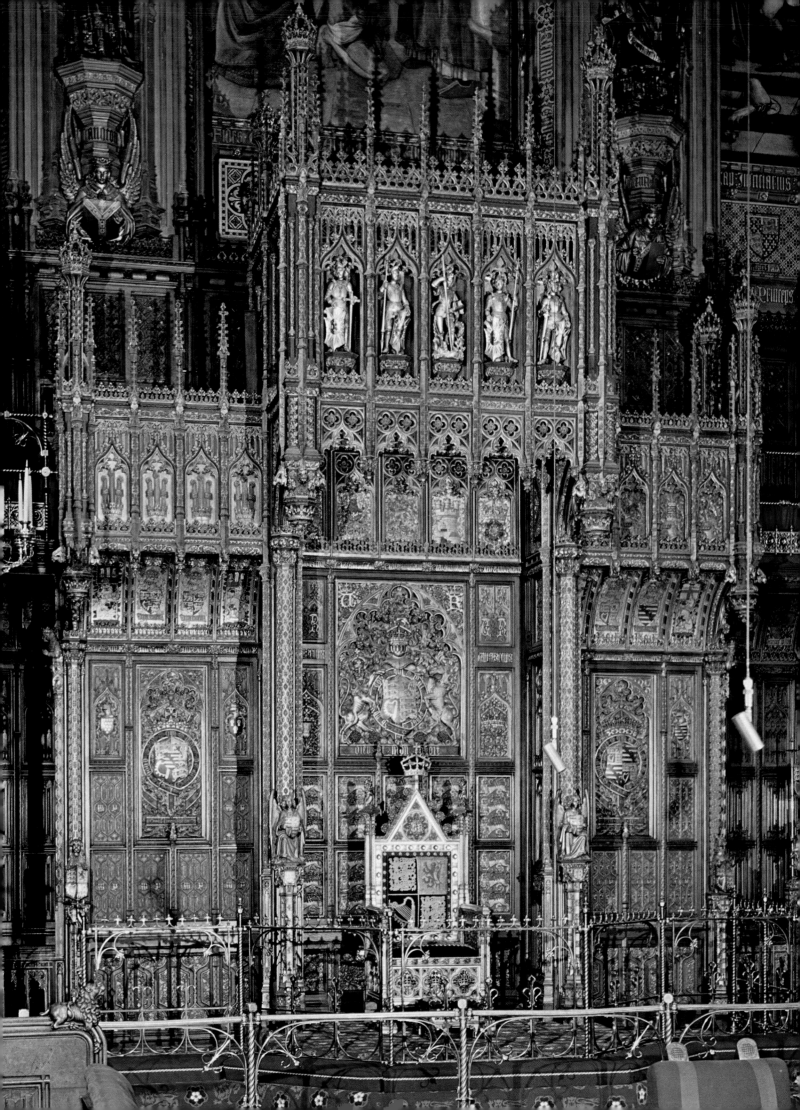

Left and right, the throne in the House of Lords. Surmounted by an elaborate canopy, it stands before a lavishly decorated heraldic screen designed by Pugin. At the center of this, above the throne, is the coat of arms of the United Kingdom (above). Other motifs in the room include the heraldic lion and unicorn (below). The crowned heads of kings and queens (below right) mark the springing of a series of arches.

WILLIAM I.

The Royal Gallery (above) connects the Royal Entrance in the Victoria Tower to the House of Lords. It is richly decorated with paintings, carvings, statues, including those of William the Conqueror (above far left), Henry V (top near left), and William III (center near left), and monumental frescoes of Wellington's victory at Waterloo and Nelson's death at Trafalgar (left). Nearby in the Prince's Chamber, a sculptural panel (right) depicts the assassination of David Rizzio, Italian counselor and favorite of Mary Queen of Scots, at the hands of Lord Darnley and his co-conspirators on March 9, 1566.

The sumptuous red and gold decor of the House of Lords is carried into the Lords' Library (above and left). The library contains thousands of volumes and offers several quiet reading rooms for the peers. A similar library is provided for members of the House of Commons.

Facing page, Westminster Hall, once the banqueting hall of the Palace of Westminster. The room miraculously survived the disastrous fire of 1834 and was later incorporated into the new Houses of Parliament. Begun in 1097 and remodeled 300 years later by the great medieval architect Henry Yevele, Westminster Hall is especially admired for its oak hammer-beam ceiling (detail, above far right), one of the oldest and largest in the world. The use of hammer beams created a lofty and airy space by increasing the possible span of the roof. From the thirteenth to the nineteenth centuries, England's chief courts of law met here.

Following page, the Speaker's residence and the clock tower, as seen from Westminster Bridge.

Houses of Parliament London, England

The tradition of parliamentary democracy in England is ancient. The "mother of parliaments," England's system of government has served as the model for democratic governments throughout the world. To the British people, their Parliament is often simply known as Westminster, after the name of the borough of London in which the Houses of Parliament are located. The pinnacled stone façade and familiar clock tower, rising on the north bank of the Thames close to Westminster Abbey, seem to symbolize the vitality of British democracy through the centuries. Yet, a disastrous fire in 1834 all but destroyed the previous buildings, and today's Parliament is in fact scarcely a hundred years old—far newer, for example, than the Capitol building in Washington, D.C.

Nonetheless, the site of the Parliament buildings has been the seat of the British government since the time of the Norman Conquest. A thousand years ago, what is now the City of Westminster was called Thorney Island. Here, where Westminster Abbey now stands, the pious King Edward the Confessor built a church, which was consecrated in 1065. To be near the church, Edward moved his court from the ancient capital at Winchester and established Westminster as the new, albeit unofficial, capital of England. In 1066, the Norman invaders under William the Conqueror seconded Edward's choice by establishing their court at Westminster, a town which was then still separate from London. The kings of England lived in Westminster for five hundred years, from 1050 until the time of the Tudors.

Only remnants of that Palace of Westminster remain, the largest and finest of which is Westminster Hall. This enormous banquet hall was begun in 1097 during the reign of William II. It was remodeled between 1394 and 1402 for Richard II by the greatest of English Gothic architects, Henry Yevele. The hall is renowned for its magnificent hammer-beam roof, which is one of the oldest and largest in the world.

The House of Lords, derived from the earlier King's Council, met in Westminster Hall, while the House of Commons eventually settled in the nearby Westminster Abbey. There the Commons gathered in the Chapter House from the fourteenth century until 1547, when it moved into St. Stephen's Chapel within the Palace of Westminster. By this time, the court had established itself in Whitehall Palace a few hundred yards up the road. The Lords and Commons eventually came to occupy the whole of Westminster Palace, where they convened until the fire of October 16, 1834, burned the palace to the ground.

Overnight the British were faced with the task of totally rebuilding their seat of government. The reconstruction was in many ways a symbolic as well as practical act, a reaffirmation of a system of democratic government that had begun its evolution six centuries earlier.

Unlike most of the countries that have formed governments based on the English model, Britain itself has no written constitution—or at least no basic text specifying the principles by which the country is governed. The Magna Carta, signed by King John in 1215, is often mistaken for a constitution. But this document was essentially a peace treaty, a compromise extracted by a rebellious and privileged social class from a king who was facing a military and financial crisis. Like many peace treaties, it was ignored almost as soon as it was drawn up.

Though the Magna Carta applied primarily to relations between the king and

Above, a thirteenth-century miniature of King John who was forced by his barons to sign the Magna Carta (left) on June 15, 1215. The Magna Carta was the first written document to limit an English king's power. Though the rights it granted originally applied only to the barons, over time it became the basis for democracy in England.

Henry VIII (right) and his daughter Elizabeth I (below). Under the Tudors, Parliament again became an instrument of the monarchy.

Simon de Montfort entered into battle against the king and took him prisoner. For a year, Simon de Montfort ruled England in the king's name. In 1265, he called a Parliament that included the first county representatives. However, the struggle for power continued, and as de Montfort suffered military setbacks his supporters began to desert him. In the summer of 1265, he was killed in battle by a band of royalists under King Henry's son, Prince Edward.

Simon de Montfort's personal ambition brought him to defeat, but the political reforms he had set in motion would have far-reaching effects. Some twenty years after he had ascended the throne, Edward convened a Parliament to which he summoned not only the customary nobles and clergymen but also called upon two knights to represent each county and two townsmen to represent each city or borough. When this body—the Model Parliament—met at Westminster in the winter of 1295, its membership included 90 churchmen, 7 earls, 41 barons, some 70 county representatives, and 200 town representatives. From that time on, members of all these classes were regularly summoned to Parliament.

Progress toward forming the representative body that exists today was slow. Many of those called to Parliament found attendance a nuisance and never went. One constituency even requested, and was granted, the privilege of not being represented at all. Nevertheless, the groundwork was being laid for a true system of national representation.

Parliament eventually became so powerful that England was pitched into a civil war between the tyrannical King Charles I and his own subjects—led by their representatives in Parliament. Charles was defeated in battle, tried before the Commons, then sentenced and beheaded in 1649. But democracy in England fared no better under his successor, the Lord Protector Oliver Cromwell; and in 1660, the monarchy was restored with overwhelming popular support. Charles II, the eldest surviving son of Charles I, was crowned king.

his barons, some of the principles it set forth laid the foundation for the modern concept of representative democracy by calling for the meeting of a Common Council to discuss the levying of certain taxes. In 1258, the barons forced the king—John's son and successor, Henry III—to agree to a new council, or Parliament, to preside over the affairs of the realm. The term "parliament" (meaning "debate" or "conference"—or, as Thomas Carlyle would later have it, "gossip shop") had previously been used to describe the irregular meetings of the king's various advisers; the new Parliament, however, was to consist of delegates chosen jointly by the king and the barons and was to meet regularly three times a year.

King Henry never accepted the principle underlying the establishment of Parliament. Yet when he attempted to rule without his council, his ambitious adviser

Left, James I presiding at the trial of those responsible for the Gunpowder Plot (1605), a Catholic scheme led by Guy Fawkes (below) to blow up the House of Lords. Below right, Charles I, who lost his life in his struggle with Parliament and its leader, Oliver Cromwell (right).

Charles was succeeded by his brother, James II, whose brief and oppressive reign ended in abdication. Parliament, more powerful than ever before, offered the throne to James' Protestant daughter, Mary, and her husband, William of Orange. Before they were crowned, William and Mary signed a Declaration of Rights which, in effect, bound them to a limited monarchy. William III and Mary II were the first English sovereigns to rule not by the grace of God but by the consent of Parliament, an arrangement that still exists today.

The fire that destroyed the old Houses of Parliament in 1834 provided a fortuitous solution to a long-standing problem. Parliament had needed larger quarters for some time, but the many traditions and memories associated with the Palace of Westminster discouraged plans for reconstruction. After the fire, there was general agreement that the new Parliament building should be built on the site of the old palace, but there was less agreement on the style in which it should be built. After much debate, a competition was announced in 1833 that was open only to designs in the Gothic or Elizabethan styles.

By the mid-nineteenth century, the rising spirit of nationalism in England had succeeded in turning architects from Classicism to the Gothic tradition. Although it was actually French in origin, the Gothic was often believed in England to be generically English; it had certainly been adapted and transformed into an indigenous style of architecture. A revival of the Gothic—with its pointed arches, turrets, and elaborate decorations in carved stone—suited the Romantic taste of the times more than the abstract and distant art of the ancients. In the case of the new Houses of Parliament, it was also generally agreed that a Gothic building would better complement the surviving portion of the original structure as well as Westminster Abbey across the road.

The competition attracted ninety-seven entries. Most entries eschewed the rather ill-defined Elizabethan style in favor of the neo-Gothic. At length the judges selected a design submitted by Sir Charles Barry, a well-known architect of Classical buildings. The design was in fact a collaboration between Barry and Augustus Pugin, a gifted and impassioned young architect and designer. To Barry's overall plan, Pugin had added copious and imaginative detail that was to make the Houses of Parliament a high point of the neo-Gothic.

The neo-Gothic of Barry and Pugin is essentially a veneer applied to the flat walls of a building that is Classical in conception. "All Grecian," Pugin said of Barry's design with contempt. "Tudor details on a Classical body." Yet the building is in accord with the genuinely medieval structures of Westminster Hall and Westminster Abbey. The decoration on the

William III (top left) and his wife Queen Anne (center left), like George I (above), owed their crowns to Parliament. Left, George I's Prime Minister,

Robert Walpole. Below, the oldest known depiction of Parliament (1624).

surface of the structure lightens its sheer bulk, as does its picturesque silhouette. One French observer was so moved that he dubbed it "fairy palace," and on its completion the czar of Russia called it "a dream in stone."

Construction began in 1840, even as Barry was still revising his designs for the façade. Both architects died before the building was completed: Pugin, afflicted with insanity, in 1852 and Barry in 1860, when the building was nearly finished. Some additional construction continued under the supervision of Barry's son for yet another ten years.

The Houses of Parliament are situated on a seven-and-a-half acre site on the banks of the Thames. The building has a fairly symmetrical gridiron plan, although Westminster Hall stands in the place that would otherwise have been occupied by the front wing on the House of Commons side. The two Houses—the Lords and the Commons—are situated to the right and left respectively of a central entrance and huge octagonal vestibule surmounted by a slender spire. At each end of the building is a tall tower—the two other asymmetrical elements—which, nonetheless, have virtually no effect on the symmetry of the plan. A long terrace overlooks the river.

The two distinctively different towers counteract the otherwise regular, horizontal lines of the broad river façade. To the left, as you look from the river, is the massive Victoria Tower which contains the Royal Entrance. The 336-foot tower was at the time of its construction claimed to be the "highest square tower in the world." Above the 60-foot-high Norman Porch which forms its base, the tower conceals nine floors of storage rooms, with two additional floors within its iron roof. Here are kept some one and a half million parliamentary documents, including the original copy of every Act of Parliament since 1497.

The more picturesque 320-foot clock tower, topped by the familiar pointed roof, houses Big Ben. The nickname of this thirteen-ton bell honors Sir Benjamin

Hall, the head of the parliamentary construction committee. Though the name Big Ben applies only to the bell, it has come to be used for the clock as well. This enormous timepiece has counted off the decades without losing or gaining more than half a second each year.

Westminster Hall is near the clock tower. Low and massive, the building measures more than 250 feet long by 65 feet wide and 90 feet in height. From the thirteenth century to the nineteenth, the chief courts of law in England met in this vast and chilly hall. Here Richard II was deposed. And Charles I was tried, condemned as a "Tyrant, Traitor, Murderer, and public Enemy to the good people of this Nation," and sentenced to death. Cromwell was inaugurated Lord Protector in the hall, and after the Restoration, his severed head was displayed there for twenty years. The hall's less gruesome heritage includes banquets and celebrations, and tennis balls have even been retrieved from among its roof timbers, suggesting that it once served as a royal tennis court.

The adjacent St. Stephen's Porch leads to St. Stephen's Hall, the upper chapel of the medieval church where the House of Commons once met. In the lower chapel of St. Stephen's, often mistakenly called the crypt, Members of Parliament may marry and have their children baptized. St. Stephen's Hall leads directly to the vaulted, octagonal Central Lobby. The lobby ceiling, lavishly decorated with mosaics, supports the central tower of the building, where a lantern hangs when Parliament sits at night. South of St. Stephen's Porch is the Old Palace Yard, where Guy Fawkes was put to death in 1605 for his part in the Gunpowder Plot, an unsuccessful plan to blow up the old Houses of Parliament. Every year on November 5, the event is commemorated across the country with bonfires, fireworks, festivities, and celebrations.

THE HORSE AMERICA, throwing his Master

The American Revolution occurred during the reign of George III (1760–1820), seen at an army parade (below) and in a political cartoon (far left). One cause of the rebellion was the fiscal policy of his Prime Minister, Lord North (left). North was the last Prime Minister who considered himself responsible to the king rather than to Parliament.

Within the Houses of Parliament are over a thousand rooms, a hundred staircases, eleven courtyards, and several miles of corridors. The names and layout of the rooms near the entrance reflect the annual visit of the queen for the State Opening of Parliament. On that occasion, the queen enters by the Royal Staircase in the Victoria Tower and passes through the Norman Porch—which is in fact not Norman at all but a work by Pugin.

From here she enters the Robing Room to put on her crown and ceremonial apparel. Rich in oak and decorations of gold and red, the Robing Room is a huge state chamber elaborately decorated in the neo-Gothic style. Here, as throughout the Houses of Parliament, the decorations reflect the influence of Pugin, whose tastes and theories virtually formed the early Victorian conception of the Gothic. Because he intended the building to be a showcase for the English decorative arts, contemporary sculpture, frescoes, paintings, and works in glass, tile, and metal abound.

From the Robing Room, the queen moves down the Royal Gallery, a hall 110 feet long, decorated with gilt statues of monarchs from King Alfred to Queen Anne. Huge frescoes depict the death of Nelson at Trafalgar and the triumph of Wellington at Waterloo. The intricate Minton floor tiles of the gallery are also the work of Pugin.

Finally, the queen reaches the paneled Prince's Chamber, which serves as an anteroom to the House of Lords. This is dominated by an imposing statue of Queen Victoria, during whose reign the Houses of Parliament were constructed, and is hung with a series of portraits of the Tudors executed by students at the government-supported school of art in South Kensington.

The red and gilt detail of the anteroom is picked up in the decor of the House of Lords. Here the peers sit on benches upholstered in red leather. In the center of the room is the woolsack. Traditionally the seat of the Lord Chancellor, it is named for and made of the material that made England's fortune long before the

George IV (above) became regent in 1811 for his mad father, George III. He was crowned king in 1820. He detested his wife, Caroline of Brunswick, and refused to have her crowned queen. A contemporary painting (right) shows his unsuccessful attempt to divorce her in the House of Lords, which then sat in the old Palace of Westminster.

country became a great maritime power. At the south end of the chamber stands the queen's throne, with its elaborate gilt canopy. From here the queen presides over the opening of Parliament and reads the speech—written for her by the party in power—which sets out the legislative program for the year.

The Bar, a low railing at the opposite end of the hall, marks off the space allotted to the Commons during the State Opening and other special joint sessions. No sovereign has been permitted to enter the other chamber, the House of Commons, since the day 350 years ago when Charles I did so with the intention of arresting some of its members.

Today the House of Commons is the true governing body, while the House of Lords is something of an anachronism. The Lords has no control over finance and only limited control over legislation. In fact, the function of the House of Lords is somewhat vague and unspecialized—at once symbolic, critical, political, and judicial.

On one hand, the elaborate pageantry and colorful heraldic display embodies

and upholds centuries of tradition. Yet the Lords also holds lively and informed discussions of public policy and occasionally makes revisions in legislation. Debates in the House of Lords are often free from the party affiliations and loyalties that can constrain their elected colleagues in the House of Commons; regarding such controversial issues as capital punishment or press censorship, the House of Lords has been known to raise the more liberal voice.

There are a large number of hereditary peers, whose numbers used to be continually augmented by the elevation of the powerful and influential. However, two-thirds of those who have inherited the right to sit in the Lords have never set foot there, and most of the others do so only infrequently. On the other hand, the life peers—deserving individuals honored with nonhereditary titles—are generally politically aware, and tend to contribute actively to the work of the House.

Great statesmen past their prime have traditionally been given a title and elevated to the House of Lords. For this rea-

Above left, Queen Victoria. Her reign (1837–1901) encompassed an era of prosperity and progress which also bore the imprint of two powerful Prime Ministers, William Gladstone (above center) and Benjamin Disraeli (above right). Below left, the House of Commons in 1858. Below right, Gladstone making a speech before the Commons. The Queen came to dislike Gladstone during his later terms as Prime Minister, for he was a Liberal and she a staunch Conservative; she even resorted to rebuking him publicly.

son, some elder statesmen, such as Churchill and Macmillan, have refused to be made peers. Churchill turned down a dukedom because he did not want "to be put in moth balls." Nonetheless, among those who have recently become lords are industrialists, financiers, and even trade unionists, including the former railway signalman Ernest Popplewell who, at the age of sixty-six, accepted a peerage as a reward for a lifetime spent in the cause of the workingman.

Though it now lacks political power, the House of Lords upholds the inherited values of the nation, plays the role of the

moral conscience of the country, and proves that the tradition of public service among the privileged is not dead. More than sixty years after its abolition was first proposed, the House of Lords continues to flourish. Indeed, a recent poll indicates that public opinion, perhaps somewhat sentimentally, still favors its retention.

The House of Commons, with its wooden ceilings and green upholstered benches, has always appeared more modest than the Lords. Destroyed in a bombing raid in 1941, it was rebuilt by Sir Giles Gilbert Scott from 1948 to 1950 in a restrained Gothic style that blends with the original. Although it looks rather tame in comparison with the opulent older sections of the building, the Commons retains its share of tradition: A green bag behind the Speaker's chair for petitions,

Right, a session of the House of Commons in 1906. After it was bombed in World War II, the House was rebuilt in a similar, if less elaborate, style.

Below, Winston Churchill, Prime Minister and leader of a coalition government throughout World War II, seen here in an R.A.F. uniform giving his familiar "V for Victory" sign.

tape in the cloakrooms for hanging up swords, and snuffboxes are reminders of its past. Daily business commences with the traditional procession of the Speaker, or presiding officer, who wears black knee breeches, gown, and wig. He is followed by the Serjeant at Arms, carrying the Mace, and the train bearer, chaplain, and secretary.

The Government party sits on the Speaker's right and the Opposition on his left. For a long time, there were only two parties, the Whigs and the Tories. Today there are two major parties—Labour and Conservative—as well as the Liberal party and a sprinkling of Ulster Unionists, Independents, and Welsh and Scottish Nationalists. Nevertheless, the formal and brief style of their debates has not changed substantially over the years. Though the actual process of governing England takes place for the most part at the Prime Minister's offices at Downing Street, the House of Commons still maintains its traditional responsibility: the debate of policy and the protection of individual freedom.

The House of Commons represents 750 years of tradition, of the patient if unsystematic search for freedom and respect for human dignity, and of the evolution of a modern democracy. It has been the stage for such political figures as Gladstone, Disraeli, and Lloyd George, and has witnessed numerous memorable utterances.

On May 13, 1940, Churchill took up the reins of government with the statement: "I have nothing to offer but blood, toil, tears, and sweat... You ask, what is our aim?... It is victory. Victory at all costs—victory in spite of all terrors—victory, however long and hard the road may be, for without victory, there is no survival."

When the burned-out chambers was rebuilt after the war, the main entrance, now known as the Churchill Arch, was left with its stones scarred by the fire. It stands as a memorial to England's "finest hour," an hour that owes its character to the common man, of whom Parliament is both a symbol and an instrument. Perhaps it was Churchill who best expressed the special relationship between the "mother of Parliaments" and the people it has represented through the ages. In 1954, on his eightieth birthday, in the presence of the queen, Churchill was presented with a portrait of himself by Graham Sutherland. The elderly statesman accepted the tribute with the words:

I was very glad that Mr. Atlee described my speeches in war as expressing the will...of the whole nation. Their will was resolute and remorseless and, as it proved, unconquerable.... It was a nation and race dwelling all around the globe that had the lion heart. I had the luck to be called upon to give the roar."

The Stadhuis

Antwerp, Belgium

The imposing and richly ornamented façade of the Stadhuis, or Town Hall, of Antwerp (preceding page) is a legacy of the Belgian city's sixteenth-century heyday, when it reigned as the banking capital of Europe and the Continent's busiest port. The Stadhuis (above right) dominates Antwerp's central square, the Grote Markt. The other sides of the square are formed by sixteenth- and seventeenth-century guild houses (above, below, and below right). These fine buildings were the organizational headquarters of the middle-class merchants and craftsmen. The guilds asserted their success and wealth by designing ostentatious house façades, an effective form of social and commercial advertising. Most notable of the guild houses is that of the Grand Arbalète (crossbow makers) dating from 1516, which is surmounted by an equestrian statue (below). Other merchants represented in the square were boot makers, cloth merchants, barrel makers, and carpenters.

Cornelis Floris' design for the Stadhuis façade employed Renaissance forms in a somewhat Gothic manner which resulted in a distinctly busy style known as Flemish Renaissance. The two wings still retain late-Gothic cross windows (left and below right).

Near right, Floris' reinterpretation of the typical late-Gothic municipal bell tower—a traditional symbol of local self-government under the Holy Roman Empire. It takes the form of a false gable, adorned with obelisks, sea gods, and winged lions. Statues on the lower course represent Wisdom and Justice. The figure of the Virgin, above them, was not added until 1585, the year Antwerp finally capitulated to Roman Catholic Spain. Antwerp's Renaissance architecture—so closely identified with the aspirations of its rising middle class—was a casualty of Spanish domination. The Stadhuis itself has often been copied, but few important or innovative buildings were constructed in the city during the troubled decades after 1566.

Far right, a statue of Antwerp's legendary founder, Sylvius Brabo, which stands atop a fountain sculpted in 1887 by Jef Lambeaux. Brabo is said to have slain a giant who terrorized seafarers approaching the River Scheldt by chopping off the hands of any who refused to pay a toll. Here Brabo is about to fling the giant's own hand into the river. Legend claims that the city's name is derived from the phrase hand-werpen, or "hands thrown away." Beneath Brabo, a sea figure rises majestically from the rocks and gracefully supports a ship on her shoulder in commemoration of Antwerp's successful maritime commerce.

Perhaps even more than the façade, the interior of the Stadhuis reflects the prosperity of Antwerp or, more accurately, the renewed prosperity of the city's powerful merchant class during the nineteenth century. The decline of Antwerp after 1585 was not really reversed until 1863, when the Dutch taxes on shipping traffic along the Scheldt were finally eliminated. The city began to grow rapidly, and extensive restorations were undertaken within the Stadhuis. No expense was spared in the acquisition of rich furnishings, crystal chandeliers, and elaborately carved wood paneling.

The entrance hall (above left) makes lavish use of a most aristocratic building material—red Belgian marble. However, the carved wooden caryatids supporting the glass roof illustrate a thoroughly bourgeois theme: Each statue represents a different branch of industry.

Antwerp's long struggle for independence is the subject of a series of nineteenth-century murals by the Belgian painter Hendrik Leys (below left). The panel on the left shows Margaret of Parma surrendering the keys to the city in 1567, when Antwerp entered the war with Spain. The right-hand panel depicts Antwerp's most glorious moment, the "Solemn Entry" of 1514, when the future Emperor Charles V swore to respect the city's liberties.

Top right, the painted ceiling of the Council Chamber, executed in 1717 by J. de Roose. The carved balustrade of the room is said to be the work of a prisoner of the Spanish Inquisition.

The Antechamber (center right) and the Conscription Room (bottom right) contain portraits by the nineteenth-century Flemish painters Wappers, de Keyser, and Van Brée. The huge fireplace as well as the sculptures on the chimney breast in the Conscription Room are also nineteenth-century additions.

Above far left, a gilded relief from the Leys Room showing the sixteenth-century port of Antwerp. The monogram on the plaque (center far left) stands for "The Senate and People of Antwerp," a direct adaptation of the motto of the Roman Republic. The ornamental fireplaces in the Stadhuis include many splendidly carved figures (below far left). A. Peters's figures decorating the chimney breast in the Conscription Room (near left) depict seven of Antwerp's medieval rulers. Above, a mid-sixteenth-century chimney breast taken from an old Belgian house. Below, one of the fine Sèvres vases in the Councilroom Antechamber.

The Stadhuis
Antwerp, Belgium

The history of Western art from the close of the Middle Ages is most often viewed as a succession of geniuses. The creativity and the individuality of these giants tend to dominate the limelight, often eclipsing or obscuring the role played by social and economic forces in setting the stage for new ideas. One notable exception, however, is Antwerp's sixteenth-century masterpiece of Flemish Renaissance architecture—its Stadhuis, or Town Hall.

Early in the sixteenth century, Flemish art already had more than its share of talent, and Antwerp itself was to produce one of the greatest of all—the painter Peter Paul Rubens. But the story of the Stadhuis cannot be told simply in terms of the individual who designed it. Rather it is the tale of a new and formidable class of citizens, a group that reached unprecedented heights of wealth and power in Renaissance Flanders.

Curiously enough, the commercial prosperity of the Flemish bourgeoisie had its origins in the medieval world's obsession with the Holy Land and the Crusaders. The knights and common folk of the region took up the cross in large numbers, and their enthusiasm, though authentic, was not entirely unconditional. Noble Flemish families, eager to raise

money to outfit their private armies, were often forced to grant their town-dwelling subjects new privileges in exchange for ready cash. City charters were strengthened and the municipalities, while still subject to the rule of the nobility and obligated to pay taxes, came to exercise fundamental control over their local system of justice and the organization of commerce. Practically speaking, this meant that the merchants of the towns were in a position to reap the benefits of the boom in trade that followed the Crusaders' return.

Needless to say, the financial rewards were not evenly distributed; some profited far more than others. But emerging alongside the new wealth was a genuine commitment to self-government and the rule of law. Of all the towns' new privileges, the most symbolically important was the so-called *droit du beffroi,* the right to raise a municipal bell tower. A tower served as an observation post in time of war, and its bells summoned citizens to arms, to business, and to all important communal events. Throughout late medieval Europe, it was the principal symbol of the right to bear arms, and the right to regulate trade—in other words, of independence. Understandably, citizens in towns across Flanders expressed their civic pride by making their bell towers, and the town halls from which they sprang, as magnificent as possible. The bell tower was a

A seventeenth-century map of Antwerp (above right) shows the mighty walls which once protected the city on three sides.

Right, an engraving by Frans Hegenberg, depicting the "Spanish Fury" of 1576, when the soldiers of the Duke of Alba massacred more than 7,000 citizens.

landmark that came to epitomize the spirit of the free merchant class.

In the ninth century, Antwerp was a cluster of houses crowded around the local castle, the Steen. From the start, the town's fortunes were linked to the Scheldt, a broad and navigable river estuary that stretched to the North Sea fifty-five miles away. A popular legend relates that a giant named Antigone once occupied a castle on the present site of the town, from whence he terrorized ship captains, chopping off the hands of any who refused to pay a toll. Finally a bold Roman sailor slaughtered Antigone and flung the giant's severed hands into the Scheldt. Thus, the story says, the site of Antigone's castle

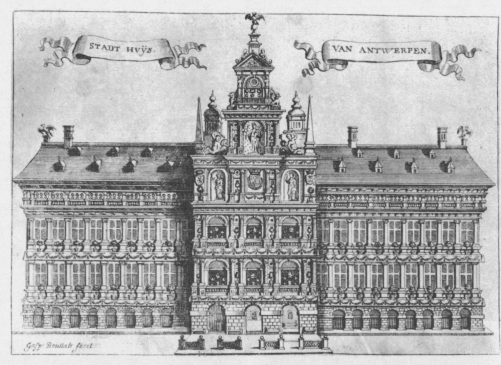

Above right, a seventeenth-century engraving of Antwerp's Stadhuis. By this time, it had already been heavily restored, after being damaged in the fighting of 1576 and 1585. Two nineteenth-century engravings show the great sculpted fireplaces in the Burgomaster's Office (near right) and the Tribunal Hall (far right). The latter is used today for weddings.

came to be known as *handwerpen,* or "hands thrown away." A less dramatic but more reliable etymology traces Antwerp's name to its location "on the wharves," or *aan't werp.*

In spite of many natural advantages, the port of Antwerp did not become important until after the eclipse of its great rival, Bruges. For many years Bruges was the economic capital not only of Flanders but also of the Low Countries, the region encompassing present-day Belgium, Luxembourg, and Holland. Moreover, as the home of artists, including the master painter Jan van Eyck, it was pre-eminent in cultural matters as well.

Then, in 1477, Charles the Bold, the young Burgundian ruler, was killed in

battle. Glimpsing the chance to be rid of the burden of its feudal overlords altogether, Flanders erupted in a series of popular rebellions. These were soon quelled by Maximilian of Austria, the husband of the Burgundian heiress. Maximilian decided that Bruges had become too powerful for comfort. Although the decline of the town was in fact already fated by the rapid silting of the Zwin River, Maximilian hastened the process. He invited foreign merchants to move their operations to the more accessible, and politically more docile, region of the Scheldt.

In the wake of this royal favor, the quietly prosperous town of Antwerp began to grow. By 1489, the German mer-

chants of the Hanseatic League had moved there from Bruges, and in 1509, the king of Portugal made Antwerp the northern headquarters of his nation's spice export trade. But the key to the town's success was its bourse, which had been opened as early as the 1460s. Inspired by the influx of foreign money, Antwerp financiers became pioneers in the development of credit and discount banking and in the use of exchange notes in lieu of cash. By 1515, Antwerp had become the undisputed financial capital of Europe.

Trade and textile manufacturing flourished in Flanders as did the arts. The Italian historian Ludovico Guicciardini, who visited the Low Countries in the mid-sixteenth century, dubbed Antwerp "truly the leading city in almost all things." Indeed, Flemish art had been in vogue in Italy for over a century. The work of Jan van Eyck of Bruges was widely acclaimed in Italy for its realism, and a number of Flemish painters were so successful abroad that they stayed in Italy most of their lives. But for every Flemish painter who remained in Italy, many more returned home, bringing with them first-hand knowledge of the Renaissance.

In the field of architecture, change was more tentative. Informal studies of Italian buildings were in circulation throughout Flanders during the early sixteenth century, but the Flemish guild system, which placed responsibility for building design in the hands of master masons, did not easily give way to the new profession of architecture. In any case, no one seemed to be able to comfortably blend the new Renaissance style with existing Flemish building forms.

Despite the awkwardness of much contemporary Flemish architecture, the wealthy merchants of Antwerp were eager to build a town hall which would reflect their prosperity—perhaps even more than their good taste. The structure of the old Stadhuis was so unsteady that "to tremble like the Town Hall" had become a popular figure of speech. Then, in 1541, a fire damaged the Stadhuis, providing a ready excuse for an ambitious rebuilding project.

Plans for the new Stadhuis, the symbolic heart of the whole municipal enterprise, progressed erratically. A competition was held inviting "both citizens and foreigners" to submit "models in stone or wood, or else drawings on parchment or paper." All the proposals received, however, were based more or less on the Gothic style, and the worldly burghers of Antwerp found them decidedly old-fashioned. Nonetheless, a design was chosen and construction began, only to be halted almost immediately.

Eighteen years later, a new competition was launched. At least ten artists submitted ground plans and models of the façade, all of them Renaissance in orientation. No document explicitly names the winner, but it was decided to begin con-

Left, the Stadhuis in 1860 and again in 1877 (below), when it was undergoing major repairs.

In 1914, Antwerp once again became the strategic target of an invading army. On October 9 of that year, the German army marched into the Grote Markt (bottom).

Through the centuries, Flemish painters decorated the interior of the Stadhuis with works celebrating Antwerp's past. Among the most notable contributions from the last century is a fresco cycle by Edgard Farasyn. The detail (above) shows an association of actors returning victorious from a contest held in Ghent in 1539.

Right, three of the twelve portraits of princes by Baron Hendrik Leys.

struction early in 1561. One of the entrants from Antwerp, a famous sculptor-architect named Cornelis Floris de Vriendt, was chosen to direct the work and make a series of plans for the Stadhuis. His Italian Renaissance and Mannerist elements clothed a traditional late-Gothic town hall, creating in the process a fresh and interesting architectural hybrid.

The Stadhuis is characterized by its arcaded ground floor, its steeply pitched, dormered roofs, and its long, uniform wings. In lieu of the customary Gothic bell tower, the Stadhuis has a tall false gable, composed of a remarkable assortment of columns, arches, obelisks, winged lions, sea gods, and statues. The whole is crowned by a golden eagle.

When it was completed in 1566, the new Town Hall was opulent enough to warm the hearts of Antwerp's free-spending citizens. Yet for all its ornamentation, the building was also dignified. It soon won recognition as the first major step in the formulation of a Flemish Renaissance style and, as such, came to be a model for new town halls in cities throughout the Low Countries.

The new Stadhuis seemed fated to preside over a long and happy golden age. In addition to its port and financial exchange, Antwerp boasted its own school of painters, fine educational institutions, and one of the most important printing establishments in Europe.

But Antwerp's peace was soon to be shattered. During the fifteenth century, the Low Countries had fallen to the Austrian Hapsburg dynasty which, under Charles V, came to rule both the Holy Roman and Spanish empires. Charles, the most powerful ruler in all Europe, had been brought up in Flanders and respected the Flemish towns' semiautonomy. When he divided his domains in 1555 between his son Philip II, as king of Spain, and his brother Ferdinand, as Holy Roman Emperor, he allocated the Low Countries to Philip. A devout Catholic and a firm believer in absolute monarchy, Philip was determined to break the independent spirit of his new possessions.

Under the harsh rule of Philip's governor, the whole region was thrown into turmoil. Executions of Protestants and Protestant sympathizers decimated Antwerp's leading families, and in November of 1576, Spanish soldiers ran amuck in the town, burning, looting, and massacring rich and poor alike.

The independence of Antwerp's burghers was broken and Antwerp itself never fully recovered. The Stadhuis, its interior severely damaged by fire, was rebuilt. Trade continued on a far more modest scale, and some families who had fled the Spanish terror returned home. Among the returning exiles was a young boy who was to spend his adolescence as an apprentice in the workshops of Antwerp's master painters. This boy was Peter Paul Rubens, a genius who would translate the unique Flemish blend of faith and materialism into the triumphant splendor of the Baroque.

The climate of Antwerp had changed dramatically. Rubens, a loyal son of Antwerp all his life, was also a Catholic, a confidant of royalty, and on occasion, a secret agent on behalf of the king of Spain. Antwerp, now the home of Europe's premier court painter, was reconciled to monarchy. But Antwerp's place as the unofficial capital of the nascent middle class, and of the increasing number of artists who catered to that class, had been lost forever.

The White House

Washington, D.C.

As the residence of the First Family, the White House has been at the center of American government and society since it was first occupied in 1800, a decade after Congress established the country's permanent capital in the forested marshes by the Potomac River. Preceding page, aerial view of the Executive Mansion looking south. Although the residence seemed needlessly spacious to its early occupants, wings were added in the twentieth century to accommodate executive functions. The northern façade (above right and below far right), which faces Lafayette Square across Pennsylvania Avenue, is the mansion's formal entrance (below center). The equestrian statue of Andrew Jackson (above) in Lafayette Square was cast in 1853 from English bronze cannon he captured in the War of 1812. Below, Ionic columns of the North Portico overlooking Lafayette Square.

Under President Thomas Jefferson the architect Benjamin Latrobe modified the original plan of 1792 for the familiar South Portico (above left) with the approval of its original designer James Hoban. The gardens of the south lawn were also laid out during Jefferson's presidency. Bottom row, left to right, details of the southern façade: a flight of stairs leading to the portico; a capital of one of the portico's Ionic columns; one of the curved pediment windows (which alternate with windows having triangular pediments); and a lantern by the south entrance. President Theodore Roosevelt added the West Wing (center right) in 1902 to separate the executive offices from the main house. The Oval Office was built in 1909 and, as the official office of the chief executive, is the most famous addition to the original structure. Top right, the southeast corner of the mansion.

Prominent visitors to the Executive Mansion are greeted in the spacious entrance hall (above) before entering the formal reception rooms on the ground floor. The Diplomatic Reception Room (left), with its "Scenic America" wallpaper printed in 1834, was the scene of Franklin D. Roosevelt's "fireside chats." The desk (1858) in the Oval Office (below) was presented to Rutherford B. Hayes by Queen Victoria.

Above right, the Cabinet Room in the West Wing where the president meets with members of his administration and Congress to formulate government policy. Below right, the large State Dining Room on the first floor. The room's decorations include gilded bronze table ornaments ordered by James Monroe in 1817 and George Healy's portrait of Abraham Lincoln, which hangs over the mantelpiece.

Each room in the White House reflects the personal and political lives of the famous families who have resided there. President Rutherford B. Hayes (1877–1881) frequently gathered with friends in his library, now the Yellow Oval Room (top). On Sunday evenings he was joined by cabinet officers and senators for hymn singing. Today, this room is still used for the First Family's private receptions, often to welcome foreign leaders.

The Map Room (immediately above) was built in the East Wing by FDR during World War II and was, in effect, the supreme headquarters of the war effort, in communication with all parts of the world. It has since been redone as a reception room with Chippendale furnishings.

The Blue Room (near right) located just off the ground-floor entrance hall, is used for state receptions. The gilt furnishings are copies of Pres-

ident Monroe's Empire-style pieces. Lining the walls are the portraits of Thomas Jefferson by Rembrandt Peale and—reflected in the mirror—of John Tyler, the tenth president, by George Healy.

The Green Room (above far right) was used from the beginning as the White House parlor. Its fireplace is one of the few surviving original fixtures in the mansion.

Lincoln's bedroom (below far right) is the only room in the White House devoted entirely to one president. The chamber served as his Cabinet Room where, on January 1, 1863, he signed the Emancipation Proclamation. A portrait of Andrew Jackson, which Lincoln admired, hangs on the wall.

Following page, an autumn view of the North Portico of the White House.

The White House Washington, D.C.

The White House may be elegant, but it is not exactly palatial. When it was first being designed, a contemporary critic complained that the United States had no need for a house "big enough for two emperors, a pope, and a grand lama," yet the White House—by international standards—has a comparatively unassuming charm. It is, after all, a house, not a Versailles. And so it is appropriate that John Adams, the first president to live in the White House, should inaugurate his stay with the following homespun prayer:

I pray Heaven to bestow the best of blessings on this house and on all that shall thereafter inhabit it. May none but honest and wise men ever rule under this roof.

The history of the White House begins with a compromise negotiated by the founding fathers in the process of selecting a permanent seat for the United States government. Contenders for the honor included Philadelphia, the temporary home of the government while the capital was being built, and a deserted area on the Potomac River near the tobacco and cotton ports of Georgetown, Maryland, and Alexandria, Virginia. In the end, Congress voted for the southernmost site, on the Potomac, as part of an arrangement which required the Southern states to shoulder some of the North's Revolutionary War debts.

The ten-mile square selected for the Federal District, or Territory of Columbia, was a swampy area, roughly divided in the center by the Potomac River. During the winter of 1791, President George Washington sent Pierre Charles L'Enfant, a French engineer and architect, to survey the district and select sites for the Capitol and the president's house. To devise a workable scheme for the sites of the proposed buildings, L'Enfant rode on horseback through wintry lowlands, woods, and marshes. He called the only rise in the district—Jenkins Hill—"a pedestal waiting for a monument" and decided that the Capitol would be built there. A mile to the northwest just above the swamp along the Tiber River, L'Enfant suggested that the "President's palace" be built on an eighty-acre plot. His plan connected the two main government buildings with a wide ceremonial route. In his design for the new capital, L'Enfant superimposed a Baroque radial plan, like that of Rome or the gardens of Versailles, on a rational eighteenth-century grid, such as that of Philadelphia or Savannah. This produced the carefully planned vistas and axes that link the monuments of the city today.

Though L'Enfant had hoped to design the president's home himself, an architectural competition was held to choose its design along with that of the Capitol. One design, ultimately rejected, was submitted by "A.Z.", who was later identified as Thomas Jefferson. In July of 1792, the Irish architect James Hoban was awarded a gold medal worth ten guineas ($500) for his winning design of the president's residence. Hoban had designed a typical Georgian country mansion 160 feet long and four stories in height. The building's hipped roof, balustrade, and alternating window arches were modeled on the Palladian architecture of mid-eighteenth-century Europe. Hoban did add a large oval room on the ground floor which is now known as the Blue Room. At the end

Far left, the winning design of the Executive Mansion by James Hoban (left). Below, Abigail Adams, who moved into the mansion in 1800 when it was still unfinished.

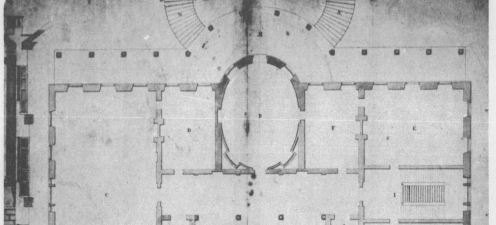

The architect Benjamin Latrobe (right) planned the first White House additions, including the North and South porticoes (sketch and plan, left). Below, Latrobe's designs of furnishings for Dolley Madison's Blue Room.

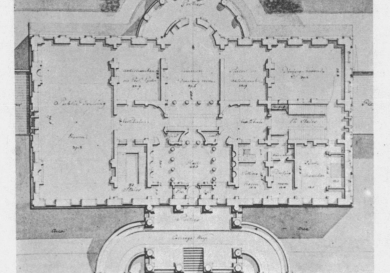

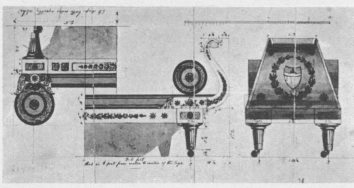

of this drawing room, long French doors opened onto the gardens on the south lawn of the mansion. He also designed a decorative American eagle in stone relief for the pediment above the stairway and main entrance.

To the left of the "elliptical salon," as Hoban referred to the Blue Room, he placed the "common dining room," now the Green Room. The long room next to it, known today as the East Room, is a traditional gathering place for guests before a reception or state dinner.

The commissioners of the Federal City had anticipated that the president's house would be completed when the government moved to Washington in eight years. By that time the entire city of Washington boasted only about forty houses, and what society the capital could claim was primarily borrowed from Georgetown. When Abigail Adams first arrived at the Execu-

tive Mansion, she wrote her daughter that "there is not a single apartment finished ...and the great unfinished audience room I make a drying room of to hang up the clothes in. The principal stairs are not up, and will not be this winter." With an unmistakable hint of sarcasm, Abigail added that it was "an establishment very well proportioned to the President's salary," which was, at that time, undeniably modest.

As John Adams soon lost his bid for re-election, it was his successor, Thomas Jefferson, who established many of the early traditions still followed in the White House. Jefferson was the first to give a gala White House reception, which took place on Independence Day in 1801. During the two-hour gathering, the president shook hands with some one hundred guests in the Blue Room—instead of bowing as his predecessors Washington and Adams had done. As president, Jefferson tried to make

the Executive Mansion a showcase of democracy but at the same time demanded fine food and tasteful entertainment. Though Jefferson considered himself a "plain" person, his accounts show that $10,000 was spent on wine during his eight-year term, a priority that didn't appeal to Mr. Adams, who complained that "Jefferson's whole eight years" were like a reception.

Jefferson commissioned Benjamin Latrobe, the English architect he had named Surveyor of Public Buildings, to design two terrace pavilions on the east and west sides of the mansion. These were completed in 1807 under the supervision of Latrobe and the original architect Hoban. Latrobe also reworked Hoban's plan for the now-famous South Portico, completed in 1824, and designed a North Portico (not built until 1929). This last included a sheltered carriageway and a Classical Revival temple front.

Dolley Madison became the White House's spirited mistress in 1808 and immediately set about adding decorative touches to her home. With $6,000 appropriated by Congress, she reupholstered furniture—much of it in yellow satin—hung damask draperies on the tall windows, and installed mirrors over the mantelpieces. Washington Irving records the "blazing splendor" of her drawing room, where she surrounded herself with the brightest of Washington society.

Dolley's early days of gracious entertaining were cut short on August 23, 1814, in the midst of the War of 1812, with word that the British army was nearing the capital. Alone in the White House, Dolley Madison wrote her sister that she had packed state papers into enough "trunks . . .to fill one carriage; our private property must be sacrificed. . . ." At the last minute she did manage to save Gilbert Stuart's full-length portrait of George Washington by ordering the frame to be broken so she could pull the portrait free. Today this historical treasure hangs in the East Room of the mansion. After setting fire to the Capitol, the British forces walked the mile to the White House, held an impromptu party with the help of the wines from the cellar, and then set the building aflame—the "blazing splendor" of the Executive Mansion was reduced to a burned-out shell.

The Executive Mansion was reopened four years later by the Monroes in the fall of 1818. Its freshly painted white walls suggested the nickname "White House," which, under Teddy Roosevelt, became its official title.

The fiery Andrew Jackson instigated radical changes in the political and social climate of the White House. Characteristically, his inaugural reception on March 4, 1829, was far from genteel. The refreshments prepared for the 20,000 persons who were celebrating the election of the "People's President" ran out, and in the crush, much furniture and china was broken.

But Jackson had known—and respected—finery at his Tennessee plantation home and, like Jefferson, was a

widower who appreciated congenial company. With nearly $50,000 appropriated during his eight years in office, he made provisions for French cuisine, planted trees, graveled walks, and installed hot and cold shower baths. Jackson also gave the aging James Hoban the opportunity to complete the East Room with the paneling and ornamental beams of the original design. Gossip mongers made much of the President's provision for no less than twenty spittoons on the list of furnishings for the renovated room. Graceful, one-story wings were added on the east and west sides of the mansion for carriages, stables, and offices.

Abraham Lincoln, the other "Westerner" who went from a "log cabin to the White House," moved into the Executive Mansion on March 4, 1861. The struggles and tragedies of Lincoln's presidency were often publicly displayed in the East Room.

Top, a White House gathering during President Rutherford B. Hayes' Administration. Immediately above, left to right, Abraham Lincoln, the sixteenth president; General Ulysses S. Grant; and a photograph of President and Mrs. William Howard Taft at the White House.

Here, a reception was held for Ulysses S. Grant—who didn't actually attend—just before he was given command of the United States Army. During the Civil War, the Blue Room was used as quarters for troops. Finally, the slain president's body lay in state on a catafalque in the black-draped room.

Despite the complications of war, the White House underwent several changes that reflected the taste and ideologies of the Lincolns. Mary Todd Lincoln redid most of the furnishings. She also convinced the president to substitute dinners with receptions, which cost much less and allowed him to greet many more people.

Lincoln opened his office two or three times a week for what he called "public opinion baths," giving the people a chance to have a private discussion with their president.

In 1902, Theodore Roosevelt hired the architectural firm of McKim, Mead, and White to design some necessary modifications that would separate the executive offices from the family rooms upstairs. The architects, who built many of the elegant homes in Newport, Rhode Island, removed the greenhouses that had been added during the nineteenth-century, exposing Jefferson's western terrace pavilions, which then became a colonnaded link between the White House and the new West Wing. This last was built so that the residents of the White House would no longer have to encounter callers waiting to see the president.

The "fireside chats" of Franklin D. Roosevelt first brought the White House close to many Americans. These radio broadcasts from the Diplomatic Reception Room on the ground floor were in keeping with FDR's thinking about the role of the Executive Mansion: "I never forget that I live in a house owned by all the American people."

By the time of Harry Truman's Administration, the White House had some structural deficiencies. Its old foundations were carrying unanticipated burdens: additional floors, heavier roofs, and modern plumbing, heating, and electricity. One evening in 1948 at a reception in the Blue Room, the Trumans suddenly noticed that a chandelier was shaking above their guests' heads—a clear indication that something had to be done. Over the next four years, a new foundation and base-

ment were built under the original outside walls, which were reinforced with a steel structure. The restorations cost nearly $5.5 million, but it was one of the few uses of public money that Americans found easy to endorse.

Since then, the White House has undergone modifications inspired by the varying tastes of the First Families. Perhaps the best known is the careful restoration supervised by Jacqueline Kennedy. True to the democratic principles upon which the White House was built, she guided the public through the remodeled White House in a television documentary. That sense of heritage was later voiced by the next First Lady, Lady Bird Johnson, when she said that "all of us share in the memories that have been accumulating here since 1800, when John and Abigail Adams first moved into this house."

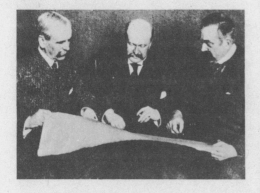

The architects McKim, Mead, and White (above) designed the White House additions in 1902 for President Theodore Roosevelt. Right, the White House, photographed in 1896. Below, the conservatories to the west that were removed when Roosevelt added to the mansion. Below right, the East Wing, built in 1942.

The Stadshus

Stockholm, Sweden

Preceding page, the Stadshus, or Town Hall, of Stockholm by the Swedish architect Ragnar Östberg. Rising above the edge of Lake Mälar, the castlelike monument is reminiscent of the Doge's Palace in Venice, but its stylistic language is based primarily on the distinctively angular Gothic and Baroque brick forms of the North. To the right of the Three Crowns Tower rise the vertical windows of the Council Hall. Built between 1911 and 1923, the Stadshus continues the centuries-old European tradition of designing town halls with towers, supremely emblematic of municipal strength and prerogative. Above, a bridge over the Klar River leading along the north façade to the main entrance.

Below far left, an inviting garden of parterres, fountains, and sculpture, which runs along the south façade past the Moon Tower.

St. George and the Dragon *(above), a statue by Christian Eriksson, is dwarfed by the 348-foot-high Three Crowns Tower (right), which is sur-mounted by the golden emblem of Sweden. The tower commands a majestic view of the islands of the Old City to the east (below).*

The diverse sculpture of the Stadshus and its gardens celebrate both man and myth in Stockholm's history. Far left, three of the best-known sculptural figures: top, Carl Eldh's idealization of August Strindberg; center, a study in bronze of a partially draped female figure; bottom, the legendary founder of the city and his prize salmon.

The anonymous universality of a contemporary sculpture (left) on Riddarholmen Island contrasts with the angular Northern style of the Town Hall. A playful water spirit (above) peers up from the bottom of a small fountain in a quiet recess of the gardens. His unruly locks are entangled with small fish and his eyes, which form the drains, can be moved from side to side.

Above right, somber historical figures in the wall niches of the Great Court, which contrast with a cherubic gilt figure of Dawn (below right). The grotto (below) is formed by an arch salvaged from the Old Riddarholmen Bridge. Within, a statue of Loki, the Norse god of discord. Here he is being punished for his mischief.

Each of the ceremonial rooms of the Stadshus was individually designed and meticulously decorated to suit its particular symbolic and practical function. The Blue Hall (top left and right) serves both as an entrance hall and festival space. Its name derives from Östberg's original intention to give the brickwork a blue wash. However, when the brickwork had been carved in situ, he liked the effect of its natural color and decided to leave it as it was.

Center left, the Prince's Gallery. This room is named after Eugene, son of King Oscar II of Sweden. The prince, who became one of the major Swedish painters of the early twentieth century, decorated the wall behind the columns with scenes of Stockholm's water life. In the window reveals are stucco reliefs by J.A.G. Acke.

The Oval Hall (bottom left), beyond which is the Prince's Gallery, was designed to display a series of eighteenth-century Gobelin tapestries from Beauvais, depicting exotic garden scenes.

Right, a flight of richly inlaid green and white marble steps leading to a gallery. It connects the Blue Hall with the Golden Chamber, which lies behind the window to the left. The organ loft of gilt wood projects from the wall above at the same height as the encircling windows.

The somewhat severe architecture of the Stadshus is enriched with specially commissioned decorative and symbolic works of art in a variety of materials. Stucco reliefs by Acke (far left, above and below) in the Prince's Gallery were molded directly on the plaster. Above near left, the carved and painted oak figure of Saint Eric, patron saint of Stockholm, based upon a thirteenth-century painting. It stands in the Aldermen's Council. In the Blue Hall, a gilt Saint George vanquishes the dragon (below near left), while the clock (above) in the vaulted Stairway of the Hundred Councilors acts out the same heroic tale twice daily. Every twelve hours, clockwork figures of Saint George and the dragon glide out of the wall to the tune of a medieval melody played on the clock bells.

Above right, a cupboard of richly sculpted oak made by Ernst Spolèn, which stands in the Three Crowns Chamber. The fanciful detail (below near right) is from one of the Gobelin tapestries in the Oval Hall. Stockholm, Queen of the Mälar (below far right) is part of a floor-to-ceiling mosaic by Einar Forseth that entirely sheaths the walls of the Golden Chamber.

Following page, the Stadshus seen across the Mälar. With its gently tapered Three Crowns Tower and the warm red of the handmade brick, it stands out proudly against the summer sky.

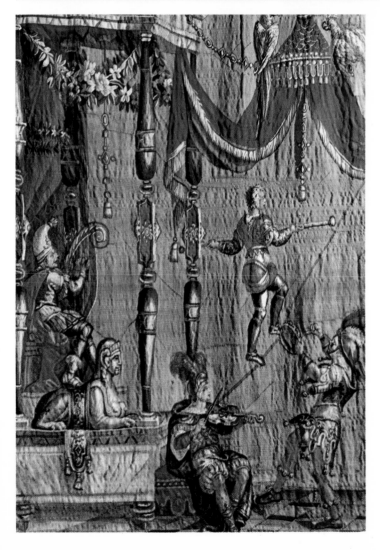

The Stadshus Stockholm, Sweden

Stockholm, the capital of Sweden, is often dubbed the "Venice of the North." Dramatically situated on several islands and peninsulas at the point where Lake Mälar flows into the Baltic Sea, it is a city of celebrated buildings and bridges set against wide reflecting expanses of water and clear skies. Unlike Venice, however, Stockholm is an open city, with broad streets and green spaces. Its waterways are used not for traffic but primarily for recreation. Every Stockholmer seems to own a boat, and during the long days of the summer months, the lake is alive with every type and size of vessel carrying picnickers and swimmers to nearby islands in the archipelago.

The most conspicuous landmark of the city is its administrative center, the Stadshus, or Town Hall, built by the architect Ragnar Östberg between 1911 and 1923. Consciously reminiscent of the Doge's Palace in Venice, it rises—massive yet gracefully proportioned—from the edge of Lake Mälar. But despite its many exotic sources, the Stadshus is a celebration of the rich heritage of Sweden and is the high point of Swedish National Romantic architecture. With its red brickwork, steeply pitched roofs, and copper turrets, it is a monument to the late-Victorian enthusiasm for craftsmanship and to Östberg's exceptional sensitivity to texture, color, and artistically worked materials.

Although there has probably been a settlement at the mouth of Lake Mälar since prehistoric times, the founding of Stockholm is attributed to the heroic Birger Jarl who ruled from 1250 to 1266 and restored national prosperity after two centuries of conflict. The conversion of the rapacious Vikings to Christianity was a violent struggle that did not end until the twelfth century. By the time of Birger Jarl, Scandinavia was impoverished and divided into petty feudal fiefdoms. To guard not only Lake Mälar but also the water routes of the Baltic and the Gulf of Bothnia against marauding pirates, and to rebuild Sweden's commerce, Birger Jarl constructed a fortress where the Royal Palace now stands in the Old City ("the city between the bridges"). Under its protection, the city grew.

Below, a print depicting scenes from the "Blood Bath of Stockholm" in 1520, when the Danish King Christian II ordered the massacre of more than one hundred of the rebellious nobles who had opposed him in 1502, under the leadership of Sten Sture the Younger.

Left, two mosaics from the Golden Chamber: Archbishop Anschar (above), who began the conversion of the Vikings to Christianity in the 850s, and Sten Sture the Elder (below), who defeated Christian I of Denmark at the Battle of Brunkeberg (1471).

Right, Gustavus Vasa, the venerated king of Sweden (1523–1560) who established lasting independence from Denmark and led his country out of the Middle Ages.

Below, a seventeenth-century map, from the atlas by the Dutch cartographer Bleau, showing the territories of the kingdom of Sweden.

The three islands of the original city, Stadsholmen (City Island), Helgeandsholmen (Holy Ghost Island), and Riddarholmen (Knights' Island), compose one of Stockholm's most attractive quarters. The old streets and buildings are interspersed with clean, enchanting little squares. Old-fashioned shops do a lively trade in antiques and attractive "junk," and there are many hospitable taverns serving traditional Swedish dishes and aquavit, a strong Scandinavian liquor.

The city, numbering only a few thousand, was still confined to this group of islands when in 1523 the young patriot Gustavus Vasa drove out the tyrannical Danish King Christian II and was himself crowned king of Sweden. Three years earlier, Christian II had claimed the Swedish throne, after the Swedish regent Sten Sture the Younger was killed in battle at Lake Åsunden. He had then ordered the massacre of more than one hundred churchmen, nobles, and burghers of the Sture party. This brutality, which has gone down in history as the "Blood Bath of Stockholm," united Sweden's rival forces under Vasa, and the Danes were routed. Vasa's reign marked the end of the Middle Ages in Sweden and the beginning of the independent Swedish state.

Some hundred years later, in the seventeenth century, King Gustavus Adolphus led Sweden into a prominent role in the Thirty Years' War and established the country as a major European power. New streets were laid out on nearby islands and on the mainland, and the island of Kungsholmen, where the Town Hall now stands, was settled. The city also grew rapidly during two later periods. The first of these came during the "Era of Liberty" in the second half of the eighteenth century, when a new constitution accorded increased powers to the Swedish Riksdag, or parliament.

Stockholm's other great period of expansion at the close of the nineteenth century came as a result of industrialization and better transportation. Because of this rapid growth, Stockholm's municipal councilors began to consider the need for a more suitable new town hall and law

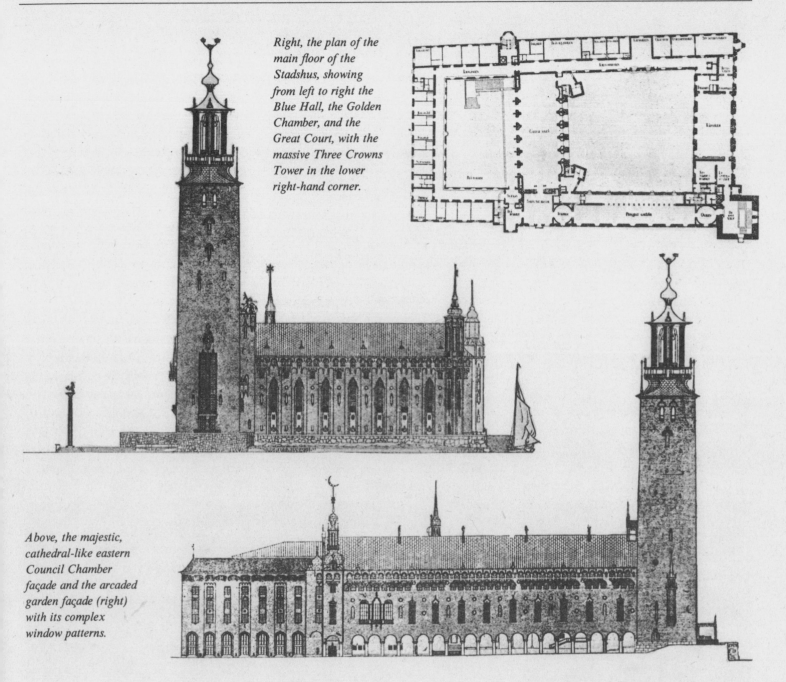

Right, the plan of the main floor of the Stadshus, showing from left to right the Blue Hall, the Golden Chamber, and the Great Court, with the massive Three Crowns Tower in the lower right-hand corner.

Above, the majestic, cathedral-like eastern Council Chamber façade and the arcaded garden façade (right) with its complex window patterns.

courts. In the preface of his book on the construction of the Town Hall, the architect Östberg quotes an old Swedish proverb, "God did not create hurry." Had the proverb not already existed, it would have been time to make it up. As he wrote: "The decision to build the Town Hall had been preceded by some fifty years of deliberation in the Town Council on the problem . . . of making a choice among the various sites proposed and the diverse designs of different architects."

Born in 1866, Östberg was a native of Stockholm. As a young man, he had often imagined solutions for this immense civic project which would be not only an administrative center but also a building that would reflect the glories of the Swedish realm and its people.

He was well-acquainted with contemporary international tendencies in architecture. At this time, the energy of the mature Arts and Crafts movement of William Morris was spreading from England throughout Europe and the United States. In Sweden itself an allied Romantic movement was discovering the native vernacular architecture, natural materials, and handicrafts.

In 1893, Östberg took a four-month trip to the United States, where he visited the Chicago World's Fair and witnessed the new collaboration developing between gifted architects, artists, and craftsmen. He also traveled from 1896 to 1899 on a fellowship to England, Europe, North Africa, and Greece. Not unexpectedly, he was concerned with the various interpretations of town halls he had seen in different countries—*hôtels de ville* in France, *palazzi communali* in Italy, *rathäuser* in Germany—each of which, he felt, "gave clear reflections of the mentalities of the diverse peoples."

Östberg won a competition in 1905 for the Municipal Law Courts, which were to be built on the shore of Kungsholmen Island facing south over the waters of Lake Mälar. But just as ground was ready to be broken, the city council changed its mind. The magnificent site was to be reserved for a town hall. Three years later, on March 27, 1911, the site was again turned over to Östberg for its new purpose. The exterior of the building is of handmade bricks, which are identical in size with those used in the palace of Gustavus Vasa. (The Town Hall was dedicated on midsummer's eve of 1923, the four hundredth anniversary of Vasa's state entry into Stockholm.) Native woods and stone were used throughout, as were historical design motifs. The tapering Three Crowns Tower rises from a symbolic stone bastion supporting a monument to Birger Jarl. The wealth of garden sculpture includes statues by Carl Eldh of the painter Ernst Josephson, the poet Gustaf Fröding, and the dramatist August Strindberg.

The building takes the form of a huge hollow rectangle divided into two unequal parts by an internal transverse wing, which contains the Town Hall's best-known room—the Golden Chamber, where the Nobel prizes are presented each year. On either side of this are the two largest spaces: the Great Court, which is open to the sky, and the Blue Hall.

The principal entrance on the north side of the building leads directly into the Great Court, where one can pass through to the municipal offices, the formal rooms of the aldermen and councilors, or the great decorated halls. Seven stories of municipal offices surround the remaining three sides of the great Blue Hall. Additional offices, as well as the legislative and ceremonial chambers, occupy the four-story wings around the Great Court.

The Council Chamber, at the east end of the building, is the heart of the Town Hall. With its tall, exposed roof structure and refined ornamentation, it reflects the dual nature of a city which combines rugged natural beauties with the advantages of civilization and culture. But it is the large ceremonial spaces—the Prince's Gallery, the Blue Hall, and the adjoining Golden Chamber—that have the greatest impact. Östberg was so taken with the color and texture of the carved red brick of the Blue Hall that it was never covered

with the blue lime wash he originally intended for it—and for which it had already been named. The hall's high horizontal windows disappear behind nonarchitectural awninglike valances. With its brick walls and marble floors, stairs and balcony of marble, the Blue Hall is stately and grand. In contrast, the adjoining Golden Chamber seems to dissolve in the brilliance of its own shimmering surfaces: From floor to ceiling, its walls are mosaicked in gold. This work of Einar Forseth terminates at the north end of the room in a huge representation of *Stockholm, Queen of the Mälar.*

Östberg worked on the Stadshus for more than twenty years. By the time it was completed, the heyday of Romantic Nationalism was over, and the architect himself was rapidly turning to a Scandinavian Neoclassicism. Stockholm's Stadshus, however, remains his masterpiece, celebrating in every detail of form and decoration the heritage of the Swedish nation.

These photographs of the south façade of the Town Hall were taken in 1923, the year the building was inaugurated. Östberg's deliberate Venetian references are seen in the window shapes and rhythms and in the arcaded portico.

City of Brasília

Brazil

Everything about Brasília verges on the fantastic. Having progressed from inception to occupancy in a frantic three-year period (1957–1960), the Brazilian capital appears at first glance more like a surreal architect's model than an active city. The symbolic center of Brasília is the Plaza of the Three Powers (preceding page), where the three most significant government buildings are situated. The National Congress Building—which includes the "flying saucer"-topped platform and bifurcated Secretariat Tower—stands at the apex of a triangle. The Supreme Court (lower left) and the Palace of the Planalto (lower right), where the presidential offices are located, form the other two corners. The many ministry buildings line both sides of the mall. The commercial and cultural district of Brasília rises in the background.

The design of the Plaza of the Three Powers was intended to represent a coequal relationship between the republic's legislative, judicial, and executive branches. The Congress Building (left, above and below) consists of two partial spheres that house the Senate Chamber and the Hall of Deputies. They rest on a vast horizontal podium of white marble that is connected to a sunken courtyard below by a long sloping ramp. Behind the Congress buildings and Secretariat Tower is the Palace of the Planalto (right). The natural savanna preserve in the background is a reminder of the daring required to create a capital city in Brazil's vast hinterland.

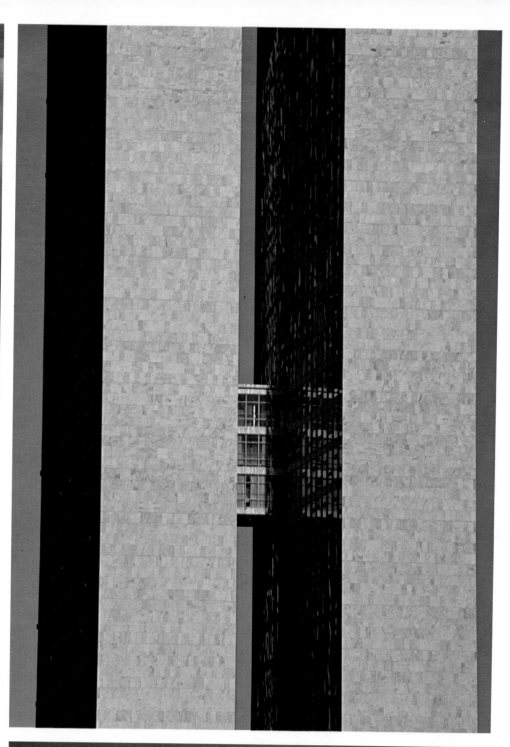

Above, Brasília's Congress Building, with the Senate Chamber at left and the Hall of Deputies on the right. Behind them rises the twenty-five-story Secretariat, where administrative offices are located. The sole connecting link between the twin vertical slabs of the Secretariat is an aerial, three-story glass bridge (above right). Right, the almost unearthly inverted dome that houses the Hall of Deputies. Over 200 feet in diameter, it rises 33 feet above its white marble base. In front of the Congress Building, in the center of the plaza, is Bruno Giorgio's huge and suitably surreal sculpture The Warriors *(left).*

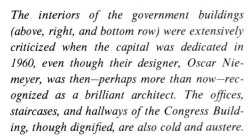

The interiors of the government buildings (above, right, and bottom row) were extensively criticized when the capital was dedicated in 1960, even though their designer, Oscar Niemeyer, was then—perhaps more than now—recognized as a brilliant architect. The offices, staircases, and hallways of the Congress Building, though dignified, are also cold and austere.

Although Brasília seems a deliberate symbolic expression of the military government now ruling the country, the city was in fact the creation of a democratically elected government, and its architecture was intended to commemorate the Republic of Brazil. The shape of the Hall of Deputies, whose graceful sculptured edge looms above the soldier (left), was meant, in Niemeyer's words, "to sprout like a symbol of the legislative power."

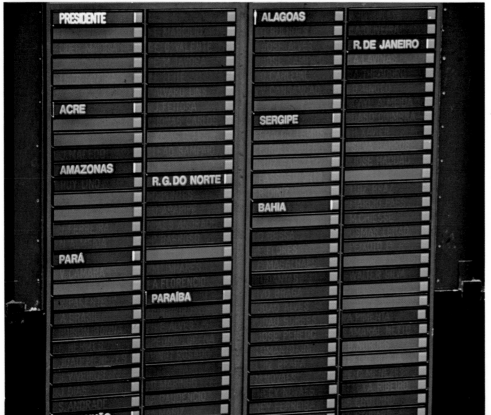

In the circular Hall of Deputies (above, left and right) the presidential desk is raised above the floor of the hall on a platform that also holds the stenographers' desks. Right, the similar but smaller Senate Chamber. Left, an illuminated voting panel in the Hall of Deputies bearing the names of the Federated States of Brazil.

At sunset the image of the Congress Building (following page) shimmers in an artificial pool, fulfilling architect Oscar Niemeyer's vision of "forms that are not anchored to earth rigidly and statically, but uplifted . . . white and ethereal, in the endless nights of the highlands, surprising and breathtaking."

City of Brasília
Brazil

In 1913, on an expedition across the South American wilderness, Theodore Roosevelt camped briefly at the western edge of the Planalto, the isolated, high central plateau of Brazil. "The air was wonderful," he wrote afterward. "The vast open spaces gave a sense of abounding vigor and freedom. Surely in the future this region will be the home of a healthy, highly civilized population."

Brasília, the city that became the realization of ·Roosevelt's prophecy, would have appalled him. Even visitors accustomed to the architectural developments of the past fifty years find it difficult to reconcile the extravagant individuality of Brasília's monumental public buildings with the relentlessly monotonous rationalism of the rest of the city.

It is perhaps too early to say whether Brasília is indeed the city of the future, as its builders claim, or the "city of Kafka," as the Italian critic Bruno Zevi has labeled it. Here is a metropolis whose inhabitants live in enormous "superblock" complexes, a city of freeways and overpasses that ne-

glects the pedestrian. "Because of the great open spaces, everything is too far for walking with a purpose," a journalist noted recently, "and the idea of strolling simply hasn't caught on here."

It may be too early, even, to think of Brasília as a city. The accidental accumulations of centuries that give a city its distinctive character cannot, of course, be manufactured overnight. Today, Brasília is still not so much a capital city as it is a bold gesture.

The man most directly responsible for this gesture—Juscelino Kubitschek de Oliveira—was inaugurated president of a then still democratic Brazil in 1956. Brazilians had been talking about establishing an inland capital as early as 1891. Little was done, however, until the administration of Kubitschek's predecessor, when the site for the city was selected. Traditionally, newly elected Brazilian presidents have disavowed the prized projects of the previous administration, and most observers assumed Kubitschek would do the same.

In the middle of his election campaign, however, a heckler shouted, "What about Brasília?", and the candidate, who had never given the issue any serious thought, proclaimed impulsively, "I will implement the Constitution!"

Once in office, Kubitschek's offhand campaign promise soon developed into an obsession. He lost no time in reviving all the old arguments for the development of the interior—arguments that, if valid in 1891, had grown even more compelling over the years. Because the world's fifth largest country had no road network, Kubitschek said, "Enormous fertile lands are as empty as the Sahara while millions of Brazilians live in penury, clinging like crabs to the shoreline. We must occupy our country."

Kubitschek had to act quickly. His term of office would expire in 1961, and he could not legally succeed himself. Unless the city was actually built and recognized as the new capital by that time, his successor would most likely disclaim the project

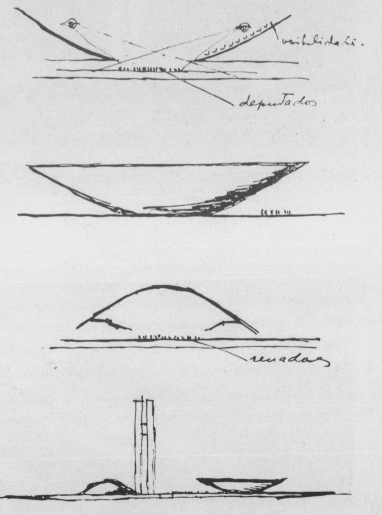

Left, Oscar Niemeyer (on the left), the architect who designed all of Brasília's major public buildings, and his colleagues during the city's rapid construction. A brilliant improviser, he was capable of designing even the major buildings of the complex in less than a fortnight.

Right, Niemeyer's preliminary sketches for the National Congress Building. Behind the two half-spheres rises the Secretariat, the only tall structure in the Plaza of the Three Powers.

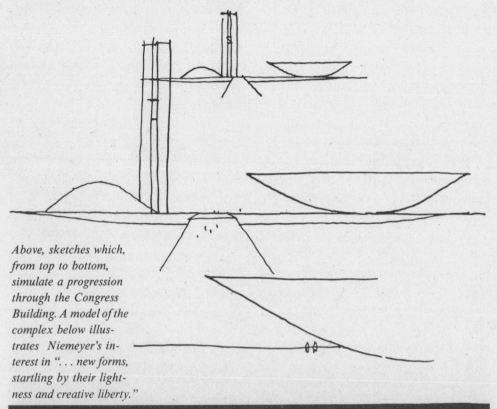

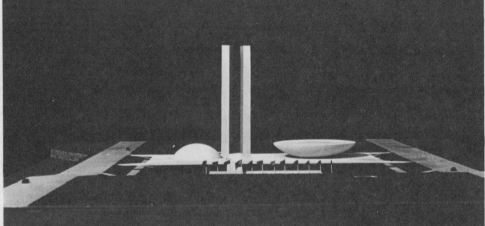

Above, sketches which, from top to bottom, simulate a progression through the Congress Building. A model of the complex below illustrates Niemeyer's interest in ". . . new forms, startling by their lightness and creative liberty."

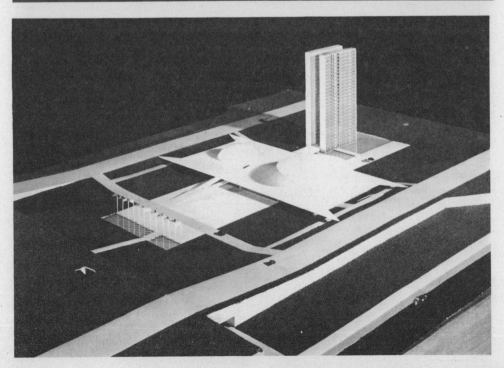

and stop work immediately. The proposed site, 600 miles northwest of Rio, was 78 miles from the nearest railroad, 120 miles from the nearest airport, and 400 miles from the nearest paved highway. Coupled with these enormous obstacles were Brazil's lack of heavy industry and its inefficient and slow construction trades. But if Brazil was backward in some respects, its architects, among them Oscar Niemeyer, had been in the forefront of modern design since the 1930s.

Niemeyer was fortunate enough to have begun his architectural career in the thirties in the office of Lúcio Costa, Rio's most influential Modernist. Costa had led the attack against nineteenth-century academicism in the 1920s and, with Niemeyer and others, had collaborated with Le Corbusier on Rio's Ministry of Education and Health Building.

One of Niemeyer's first big opportunities to work on his own came in 1941 with the commission to design a recreation complex at Pampúlha, a suburb of the city of Belo Horizonte. Given liberal guidelines, the young architect seized the opportunity to experiment. In the process of designing the complex, Niemeyer turned from the doctrinaire functionalism of the orthodox International style to an almost lyrical freedom of expression. Le Corbusier told him, "You're doing Baroque with reinforced concrete, but you're doing it very well."

With the project at Pampúlha behind him, Niemeyer's international standing as a virtuoso designer was assured. He was known as a brilliant improviser who could sketch out a complete building design overnight. Details didn't interest him and his nonchalance sometimes had unpleasant consequences for his clients. In designing the Gambling Casino at Pampúlha, for instance, he forgot to include a kitchen, and the owners had no choice but to squeeze one in after the building had gone up. Somehow Niemeyer's reputation, which was based more on his poetics than his plumbing, survived intact. As he put it, "Architecture is not just a matter of engineering, but an exteriorization of the mind."

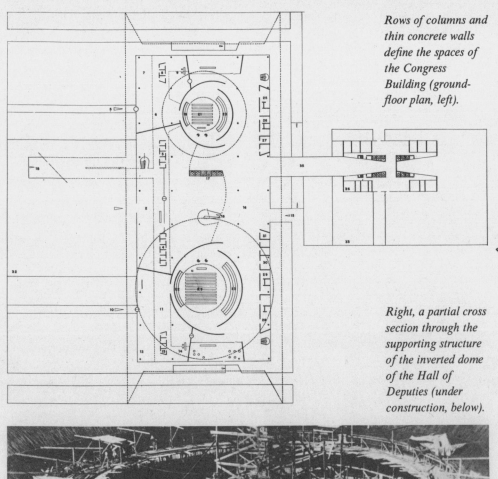

Rows of columns and thin concrete walls define the spaces of the Congress Building (ground-floor plan, left).

Right, a partial cross section through the supporting structure of the inverted dome of the Hall of Deputies (under construction, below).

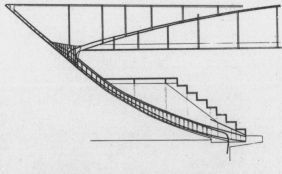

lined with ranks of government buildings. At the nose of the airplane would rise the Plaza of the Three Powers, a triangular space defined by the National Congress Building, the Supreme Court, and the Planalto Palace housing the presidential offices. Costa intended this arrangement to symbolize the equality of the legislative, judicial, and executive branches of the federal government. The more than four-and-a-half-mile mall—flanked by the vari-ous ministries, a cathedral, and a cultural center—would terminate at a municipal square, bounded by the Town Hall and other civic offices.

As soon as Costa's plan was selected, construction began at a frantic pace. Niemeyer had only three years, one month, and five days until the formal inauguration of the city was to be held. His ability to improvise manifested itself at once. As Niemeyer himself later recalled, he "had to draw in a fortnight plans that normally required two or three months."

Kubitschek's enthusiasm for the new city was not unopposed. There were many who thought the president was mainly interested in building a monument to himself. Newspaper editorials called him "Pharaoh Juscelino" and compared him to the Egyptian Pharaoh Amenhotep IV, who built a new capital city, Akhetaton, after deciding that Thebes was out of favor with his god. Kubitschek was undaunted. Sixty thousand workers were ultimately brought to the capital site, and the skeletons of the ten-story ministry buildings went up in periods as short as eighteen days. In 1958, Niemeyer moved to the site so that he could direct operations full time from a construction shack. In an adjoining room, two dozen drafts-

Inevitably, Kubitschek chose Niemeyer to design Brasília's major buildings, and the architect immediately abandoned his lucrative private practice to become the $300-a-month consultant for NOVACAP, a government corporation formed to carry out construction of the capital. Kubitschek also wanted his old friend to plan the city by himself, but Niemeyer felt that NOVACAP should sponsor a competition to find a plan.

Twenty-six individual designers and firms entered the competition. One entrant, Niemeyer's old mentor Lúcio Costa, merely submitted a few ideas sketched on five medium-sized cards accompanied by a brief memorandum. When the results of the competition were announced in March of 1957, one of the jurors noted that "all great plans are fundamentally simple.

They can be appreciated at a glance." The jury had selected Costa's.

In his own words, the design "was born of that initial gesture which anyone would make when pointing to a given place, or taking possession of it: the drawing of two axes crossing each other at right angles." The shape formed by Costa's two axes has been described variously as a bird, a dragonfly, and that predominant symbol of the modern age, the airplane. The wings of this airplane would stretch north and south along a motor freeway bordering an artificial lake. Here, Brasília's inhabitants would live in huge apartment "superblocks." These blocks, each with its own shops, schools, and hospital, would serve in lieu of neighborhoods. The center of the city's east-west axis—the fuselage of the airplane—would be laid out as a great mall

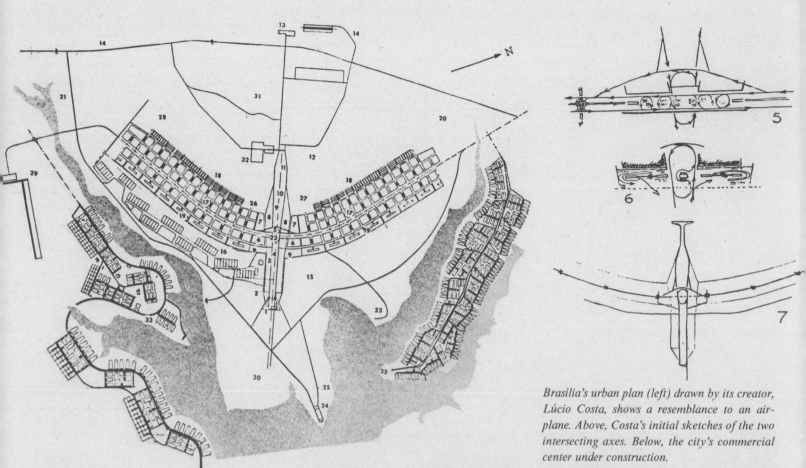

Brasília's urban plan (left) drawn by its creator, Lúcio Costa, shows a resemblance to an airplane. Above, Costa's initial sketches of the two intersecting axes. Below, the city's commercial center under construction.

men executed Niemeyer's ideas. Characteristically, the builders often had to sweat over design details that made light of the realities of construction so that Niemeyer was daily required to make dozens of on-the-spot decisions.

On April 21, 1960, in a ceremony that included a joint session of congress and a display of thirty-eight tons of fireworks, the city was formally dedicated. Much work was still unfinished, but the major government buildings were occupied by their ministries, and ninety-four apartment blocks were ready to accommodate at least some of the relocated bureaucrats. "We have turned our back to the sea and penetrated to the heartland of the nation," Kubitschek announced. "Now the people realize their strength."

Nonetheless, the debate continues: Was it worth it? Visitors to the capital have found evidence of shoddy workmanship and, Niemeyer's reputation notwithstanding, many fault much of his work for being mechanical and unimaginative. What's more, Kubitschek's obsession imposed a substantial additional burden on Brazil's economy. Between 1956 and 1961, her already large foreign debt nearly doubled and the cost of living tripled. Such personal hardship for the country's citizens undoubtedly contributed to the chaos that culminated in the 1964 overthrow of Kubitschek's democratically elected successor by a military dictatorship.

One of the strongest attacks comes from those who argue that, while Brasília was intended as a bold monument to the country's future, its antiseptic modernity seems contrary to the lively national character of the Brazilian people. Their charm and warmth are still best observed in the crowded, colorful—and disorganized—streets of Rio. Yet the Brazilians themselves, whatever they may think of the regime that now occupies it, are proud of Brasília. Foreigners should perhaps be cautious in judging the appropriateness of another national capital. After all, it was decades before Pierre L'Enfant's grand design for Washington, D.C.—another artificial new capital city based upon foreign ideas—finally began to look "American."